Barbara Greene was born in Brazil and educated at Sidcot School in Somerset. She is the widow of Count Rudolf Strachwitz, former German Ambassador to the Vatican, and now lives in Munich and on the island of Gozo, Malta, where she devotes her time to helping the handicapped, the blind and the deaf. She has published several books, including *Valley of Peace, the Story of Liechtenstein* (in English and German), *God of a Hundred Names*, together with Victor Gollancz (first published in 1962 and still selling steadily) and *The Chance of a Lifetime*, published in the USA. Barbara Greene (Countess Strachwitz) has two children and five grandchildren.

# TOO LATE TO TURN BACK

Barbara and Graham Greene
in Liberia

## BARBARA GREENE

With an Introduction
by Paul Theroux

PENGUIN BOOKS

PENGUIN BOOKS

Published by the Penguin Group
Penguin Books Ltd, 27 Wrights Lane, London w8 5tz, England
Viking Penguin, a division of Penguin Books USA Inc.
375 Hudson Street, New York, New York 10014, USA
Penguin Books Australia Ltd, Ringwood, Victoria, Australia
Penguin Books Canada Ltd, 2801 John Street, Markham, Ontario, Canada l3r 1b4
Penguin Books (NZ) Ltd, 182–190 Wairau Road, Auckland 10, New Zealand

Penguin Books Ltd, Registered Offices: Harmondsworth, Middlesex, England

First published, under the title *Land Benighted*, 1938
This edition, with a new Foreword by Barbara Greene and a
new introduction by Paul Theroux, first published by Settle and Bendall 1981
Published in Penguin Books 1990
1 3 5 7 9 10 8 6 4 2

Printed in England by Clays Ltd, St Ives plc

To all my dear friends past and present
but particularly to
Amadu, Laminah, Cook and Mark

# ACKNOWLEDGEMENTS

I would like to express my sincere thanks to the Hon. Mrs. (Julia) Stonor, Mr. Paul Theroux and my cousin Dr. Raymond Greene for their help, encouragement and patience.

# FOREWORD TO THE NEW EDITION

Almost fifty years have now passed since my cousin Graham and I set off so confidently and so ignorantly to walk through the jungles of a country that we knew almost nothing about. Liberia was indeed unexplored territory. Neither Graham nor I had been to Africa before, nor had we ever attempted a similar expedition. We were two innocents, our ignorance was abysmal, and we had no maps—because there were none. I was then twenty-three and Graham about five years older.

At that time Graham and I hardly knew one another, even though we had grown up in the same town. Graham's father, Charles, was the headmaster of Berkhamsted School. He had a brilliant intellect and had originally intended to become a barrister, but he had taken on a temporary job at Berkhamsted while waiting to 'eat his dinners', found that he had a talent and a liking for teaching, and simply stayed on. His brother, my father, was very different. He had been removed from school at a rather early age as he was considered to be not at all clever. The eldest brother, Graham, was almost as brilliant as Charles but in a different, hard-working and conscientious, style, and he ended his career as Permanent Secretary at the Admiralty. But my poor father, instead of going to a university, was put on a farm by his despairing parents in the hope that he would somehow be able there to make up his mind as to what he intended to do with his life. During his year on the farm he developed an intense love of country life and an inferiority complex, and he suddenly decided that somehow he simply must go off, far far away. By chance he came across an article in some newspaper describing Brazil as the country of the future, and on the spot he decided to go there. He was right to do so. He very soon discovered that he had a genius for business and a true pioneer spirit, and for the rest of his life he loved Brazil. He was successful and became very prosperous and at the age of thirty-four he married my mother, who had just turned seventeen.

My mother's parents, who were German, had emigrated to Brazil. By far the youngest of six daughters, she had been brought up in Brazil and had even attended a very select Brazilian boarding school, the only non-Brazilian and non-Catholic child there. She was greatly pitied by her fellow pupils when they discovered, when she was fourteen, that her parents had not yet selected her future husband and they told her that she would surely end up an old maid. She wrote a charming account of her life at this school and was persuaded to read it over the British radio when she was in her eighties.

My father brought my mother to England after their marriage and this shy young bride, so used to a very different kind of life in Brazil, was suddenly surrounded by swarms, literally swarms, of Greenes, all of them full of energy and artistic and literary interests, and all of them perfectly convinced that the British way of life was the only true and right one, and firmly determined to teach her this lesson. It could not have been easy for her but she was young and adaptable and too busy with other things to be unhappy. By the time she was twenty-one she had had three children and, after a few years, she had three more. I was the eldest of the second batch.

My father then bought The Hall at Berkhamsted because by this time he had become great friends with his brother Charles, who had married a beautiful cousin and was producing the same number of children, corresponding in age more or less to our family. My cousin Graham belonged to the older group while I was in the lower category, and somehow there was always something of an invisible dividing line between the two groups, though of course we were constantly meeting at family parties, surrounded by endless relatives, and the nurses and governesses one had in those days. I remember my mother saying at the end of one summer that we had never been less than sixteen at table. That, of course, applied to lunch; we children were nearly grown up before we were allowed to come down to dining room dinner.

The nursery regime, both in my family and in Graham's, was a strict one and we had hardly any pocket money. Punctuality, bed-times, prayers, and church on Sundays were immovable milestones, but on the other hand we—especially at The Hall—had huge gardens (a rose garden was specially laid out in memory of the gardeners who fell in World War I), ponies, tennis courts, a home farm (where we learnt to milk cows) and endless servants, who adored my mother and never left. There was always something going on; the gardens were thrown open at times for fêtes and garden parties in aid of charity, and our maiden aunts were constantly writing plays and pageants for us to act in. We all learnt a musical instrument and got up our own band, singing songs round the piano. Graham kept rather away from these activities at The Hall. His family were not musical, laying more emphasis on books, and reading became an important part of their lives. They were known as the intellectual Greenes and were always far better at school than any of us.

The Hall no longer exists. A housing estate now covers the entire property. But Berkhamsted School and the house where Graham grew up are, I believe, more or less as they were then, though the school has grown in numbers and there is now a 'House' named 'Greene House'.

My father was not unique in our family in having a keen business sense. One of his uncles was Governor of the Bank of England; his town house was in Millionaire's Row in Kensington and is now the residence of either the Russian or the Japanese Ambassador. The numbers have been changed so it is hard to identify it. My shy young mother had to endure many very long, heavy and boring lunches there, after which 'carriage exercise' was taken round and round Hyde Park, only to return to long and boring teas. Great Uncle Benjamin left his millions to his only surviving child, an unmarried daughter, who, in her turn left half of it to a missionary society (on the condition that none of the missionaries were to receive any medical training whatsoever but only to preach the 'pure word'), and the other half to a home for lost cats. I have a beautiful fan that belonged to her.

The family fortunes came at that time chiefly from large sugar estates in St. Kitts in the West Indies. Various young members of the family—even boys of sixteen— were sent out to manage these estates, far from friends, far from any white companions, where they led sad, lonely lives until they died, usually at an early age. My grandfather (and Graham's) died out there of yellow fever when on a visit. But the estates failed when sugar beet began to be grown in Europe and not even the mansion is left, though it is said that some of the local inhabitants have traces of Greene blood.

So it was that Graham and I had a more or less similar upbringing in our earliest years. I think Graham's chief friend was my older brother and they went off for long and completely silent walks together. The gap of five years—so important in childhood—kept us strangers, and then of course we were later sent off to our boarding schools: Graham to Berkhamsted, which was difficult for him with his father as headmaster, and I to Somerset, for some unknown reason to a Quaker school, a school of such austerity as would not be tolerated to-day, but where I was supremely happy.

My father's year on the farm in his early youth turned into a lifelong interest, and while he continued to go back and forth to Brazil, sometimes taking some of us with him, he also bought a property at Little Wittenham, near Oxford, which he turned into a model farm. We were there a lot in the summer and at week-ends, but although Graham spent three years at Oxford I do not remember ever meeting him there. Later, when his brother Hugh was at Merton, I joined the university social life and he brought his friends to Little Wittenham. My eldest brother had been at Oxford but I had been a schoolgirl at the time, and my two other brothers went to Cambridge.

My parents also had a flat in London, but we were rarely allowed to go there except for visits to the dentist or for educational expeditions to museums, concerts or occasional theatres. Later, when we were all grown up, The Hall was sold and my father bought a house in Montagu Square which became my mother's favourite home. I saw practically nothing of Graham for some years. He had married young and was busy building up his own life. My father suffered severe losses in the financial crisis of the early thirties, but by that time he was used to his own ways and there was little alteration in our style of life till World War II changed the old order for ever everywhere. Mercifully for him my father died in 1937.

Graham's and my adventure together began when we met at the wedding reception of his brother Hugh, where we were all merrily drinking champagne—I think that was in 1935. Graham had already made his plans for going to Liberia. Travel books to out-of-the-way places were popular at that time, Graham had a family to provide for, and his publisher had advanced him the money for a new book. From childhood on he had enjoyed adventure stories and unknown Liberia sounded hopeful, but he did not like the idea of going alone. He was trying to persuade someone, anyone, to go with him, and only after everyone else had refused did he ask me and I promptly agreed to accompany him, though I had no clear idea of exactly where he was going to.

Next morning we both rather regretted this champagne decision, I because I was enjoying myself very much in London just then, and Graham because his heart sank at the thought of having to be responsible for a young girl he hardly knew. I told him on the telephone not to worry, my father would certainly forbid it. But now came what was perhaps the most unexpected part of the whole enterprise. 'Papa' I said timidly, 'I've done a very silly thing. I've told

Graham I'd go to Liberia with him.' My father, after only a moment's pause, answered quietly but firmly: 'At *last* one of my daughters is showing a little initiative.' There was never any arguing with my father and Graham was quite in despair. He sent me endless hair-raising reports of conditions in the interior, lists of unchecked diseases, accounts of savage campaigns by local tribes and anything else he could lay his hands on. But he, as well as I, knew that there was really nothing we could do but accept the verdict, and in a fortnight we were on our way.

Whatever qualms Graham may have suffered, I think that my own reaction was chiefly one of excitement. Everything sailed along so quickly and perhaps I was also a little flattered by the attentions I was receiving. It was unusual then for young girls to adventure off into the wilds—but my father was in many ways an unusual man. Apart from getting my visa and some injections, I really had nothing else to do. I am ashamed now to admit that I had no idea how much work was needed when preparing for such an expedition, how the question of medical supplies (among a hundred other things) had to be gone into with great care, though that proved later to have been rather wasted work as nearly all our medical supplies were left behind in Freetown in the final rush. Graham saw to everything and I felt sure that he knew what he was doing, though I now wonder whether I really thought about it at all. Even my father, after giving Graham a cheque, seems to me now to have taken everything most casually. My path had always been cleared for me by others and I took it for granted. It was only later in the hard school of life that I finally learnt that help did not just fall like the gentle dew from heaven and that true results could be achieved only by personal effort and, more often than not, by hardship.

Graham and I were both rather shy people; as I have already said, we were really only acquaintances when we set out together and—strange though this may seem—we were still not more than friendly acquaintances when the long journey came to an end after three months. Even under the worst conditions we were invariably polite and courteous to one another; we never argued. If we disagreed on any subject we dropped it immediately, partly because the heat and sheer exhaustion drained all surplus energy. That was probably a good thing, for although it led to long silences the silences never became bitter or resentful. Graham took all the decisions and made all the plans. I merely followed. Looking back now I realize also that I was never, at any time, in the least bit helpful, but on the other hand I never, never complained. We got on well, respecting and liking one another, but when at the end we parted to go our separate ways, we said our friendly good-byes with none of those hugs and kisses so common now, and we did not meet again for months—or was it even for years?—though we were always delighted to see each other when it happened.

What, I sometimes wonder, did that journey bring me? Did it enlarge my horizons, change my ideas or character? Unconsciously I suppose it must have done, as till then I had floated lightly on the surface of what I now realize was a very privileged existence, and I remember clearly how Graham's wider experience of life and his independent views often amazed and astonished me; but how far they changed me, or how much the journey itself changed me, is now hard to judge for I was at the age when every day opens new windows to wider views. That I was forced to stick through all difficulties to the end showed no particular merit on my part, for we soon reached the point of no return. The journey brought to Graham an intense love of Africa that has never left him and he returned there whenever an opportunity offered itself. The paths of my varied life took other directions, with many ups and downs and long stretches of nothingness when I learnt to develop whatever inner resources I might have in order to keep going. I was never able to return to Africa again. Nevertheless ever since those days I have kept in my heart a dream of pure beauty and peace, a vision of moonlit villages in the jungle, friendly people dancing to the twang of a native harp and the beat of a drum, simplicity where material values were of no account and where understanding could be reached without words. In dark moments I needed only to remember those evenings and I was immediately filled with gratitude that I had been given the gift of life and the opportunities to experience such rare moments. That, I suppose, is the treasure that I brought back from my journey through Liberia.

The account I wrote of the journey was never meant for publication. Graham had already published his *Journey Without Maps*, which was not a straightforward travel book but became a more abstract account of a journey into the interior of life itself, far deeper and more complicated than anything I was capable of doing. Throughout the trip I had kept a diary in which, however weary I felt, I recorded the events of the day in some detail. When, a few years after our return to England, my father became seriously ill, I rewrote the notes I had recorded (keeping strictly to the truth) and made them into something I could read to him every morning to amuse him and keep his mind off his troubles. It was by chance that the manuscript fell into the hands of a publisher, who insisted on bringing it out exactly as I had written it. No facts were ever verified, nor were the local customs that I had so blithely and ignorantly recorded.

Half a century is a long time and events are changing the form of the world so rapidly that little remains, materially or intellectually, either in Europe or Africa, of life as we knew it in my young days. Much that was beautiful has been swept away in the process, but out of the turmoil of the present time a new and, let us hope, a better and fairer order will be born. At my age I can only be a spectator but I hope to live long enough to see the new shape of the world to come. In these fifty years naturally I too have changed and surely Liberia is no longer what it was then. I wish I could go back and follow the same path once again—but even if I were capable of the effort, it has often been said that one should never return to where one has once known happiness.

If this book should ever fall into the hands of any Liberian, I beg him to be kind and generous and to pass over all the inaccuracies and shortcomings, remembering that it was written by a very young girl who nevertheless would like at this late date to say a sincere 'thank-you' for some perfect memories.

Barbara Strachwitz
June 1981

Our laundry en route

The market at Bolahun

The little tart near Bassa Town

Monrovia 1935

The other passengers on the David Livingstone

Graham walking ahead after we left the Frontier

Our Cook

Graham's boy Amadu

# INTRODUCTION TO THE NEW EDITION
## by Paul Theroux

'I HADN'T even realised that she was making notes,'
Graham Greene wrote in his 1978 Introduction to
*Journey Without Maps*, 'I was so busy on my own'. And the
reader looks in vain for a portrait of Barbara Greene in
that book. She is named once, and mentioned ('my cousin
. . .') only eleven times in 300 pages. She is not important
to the narrative; she hardly exists. Once, on the way to
Bamakama, the cousins are separated. In Graham
Greene's telling this is an incidental anxiety in a couple of
paragraphs; in Barbara's it is six pages, something
approaching adventure, before—in what is a sheer coin-
cidence—the cousins bump into each other in the thick
bush. We never see Barbara Greene's face in *Journey
Without Maps*, we never hear her voice. This was deliberate. Graham Greene wanted to avoid 'the triviality of
a personal travel diary' by making it profoundly personal,
filling it with 'memories, dreams, word-associations', and
so allowing it to become metaphorical and akin to fiction.
'We share our dreams,' he wrote, and it is true that our
most powerful dreams are of wild places; the land of
dreams—or nightmares—is pretty much unmapped.

It was for both a brave trip. They were young enough
not to be intimidated by the risk they were taking.
Graham was thirty-one, Barbara was twenty-three. The

year was 1935, but the most detailed book on Liberia—Sir Harry Johnston's—had appeared thirty years earlier. The map of Liberia was blank—some rivers indicated, a few coastal towns, and the interior marked *Cannibals*. What was the appeal, then, of an exhausting journey along jungle tracks? Graham listed the attractions in his own book: it was a black republic, pledged to liberty and progress; it was brutal, disease-ridden and almost unknown to Europe; it was dark; it was the past. The lingo of Liberian politics was grandiose, but the political facts were of massacres and plagues. There was something seedy about the place: 'seediness has a very deep appeal . . . It seems to satisfy, temporarily, the sense of nostalgia for something lost; it seems to represent a stage further back'.

Graham went because of the risks and discomforts. He was not seeking self-destruction—that would have been pure folly—but self-discovery. In the Thirties, English writers 'were inclined to make uncomfortable journeys in search of bizarre material', but Graham rejected Brazil, Europe, the mapped parts of Africa, and he turned his back on an Intourist ticket into 'a plausible future'. He wrote, 'My journey represented a distrust of any future based on what we are'. But it would be wrong to see his motives as especially high-minded or inspired by the possibility of allegory. He clearly liked the idea of utter awfulness, of perhaps getting lost, of being out of touch (at a time when so many writers wanted to be in touch). He was physically strong and had a growing reputation; he was confident; throughout the early parts of *Journey Without Maps* one senses that the author is seeking adventure, and to hell with the comforts of literary London.

So far, so good. But he did not go alone.

Barbara Greene is Graham's first cousin. While Graham is elusive and even somewhat fictionalized in his own account of the journey through Liberia—as if glimpsed from between the dense overhang of tropical jungle— Barbara is completely straightforward. She is modest and a bit self-mocking; Graham led, she followed—sometimes miles behind. She left all decisions to her cousin. This was an age when men were expected to take command. Graham dealt with the carriers, the cook, the immigration formalities, the bad tempers, the disputes. It must have been a great strain—the strain certainly shows. What started as something of a lark, turned out to be an obsession; and, a critical moment, it was Graham who fell ill and was near to dying of an obscure fever. To give him his due, Graham did not make much of this near-fatal illness—'A Touch of Fever' that chapter is called—and there is no self-pity and little self-regard in *Journey Without Maps*.

*Too Late to Turn Back* is quite a different pair of shoes. It is the book that Graham wanted to avoid writing, and at the time he admitted to being 'disappointed' that Barbara wrote it. After Graham's almost Conradian push through the African darkness, how deflating it must have seemed when his companion in this trek revealed herself as a pretty young thing, not really a hiker ('I love my creature comforts'), who agreed to walk across Liberia ('wherever it was') because she was a bit tipsy on champagne. She is almost at pains to portray herself as the 'Oh, dear!', 'What a muddle!' and 'Mustn't grumble!' sort of travelling companion, though this could hardly have been the case. When her book appeared in 1938, reviewers remarked on Barbara's pluck. It seemed to be full of the sort of details which, if concerned with another place or time or companion, might have been regarded as trivial. Unlike Graham's, there were no flashbacks to Riga or Nottingham, no quotes from Baudelaire or Eliot. Graham had Burton's *Anatomy of Melancholy* in his luggage; Barbara had Maugham and the stories of Saki. It is a wonderfully telling fact, and as the trip wore on Graham became more melancholy and Barbara began to sparkle like a lighthearted deb in a Saki story. After weeks in the bush, they come upon a small black schoolmaster, one Victor Prosser, who wears 'short artificial taffeta trousers in a delicate shade of mauve'. Mr Prosser asks Barbara to describe London. She tells him about the underground railway and then is sorry she has done so:

> It all sounded horrible, and I almost felt that I did not want to go back—till, of course, I remembered Elizabeth Arden, my flat, and the Savoy Grill.

Notice that Saki-ish 'of course'.

What might have seemed trivial or unimportant about *Too Late to Turn Back* in the Thirties, now—over forty years later—is like treasure. What if Waugh had had such a companion in Abyssinia, or Peter Fleming's cousin had accompanied him to Manchuria? What if Kinglake, or Doughty, or Waterton had had a reliable witness to their miseries and splendours? We would not have thought less of these men, but we would have known much more of them.

Graham had a little twitching nerve over his right eye. When he felt particularly unwell it would twitch incessantly, and I watched it with horror. It fascinated me, and I would find my eyes fixed upon it till I was almost unable to look anywhere else. I did not tell him about it, for I got to know it so well that I was able to gauge how he was feeling without having to ask him. The social details which Barbara gives about herself—the longing for the Savoy Grill, and smoked salmon and a manicure—fix that aspect of the book in a particular time and give it its privileged pre-war flavour. The trivial, after a time, becomes revealing and even necessary, which is why we put the hairpins and buttons of Roman matrons in museums. But more important than this are the two chief virtues of *Too Late to Turn Back*. The first is that it is an intimate portrait of Graham Greene as a young man in a foreign country. It is the quintessential Greene; the Thirties were a time for him of almost manic energy, when he still believed that 'seediness has a very deep appeal' and wrote the books that made his name a resonant adjective. That Greene mood is the mood of *Journey Without Maps*. The other virtue, but it is unintentional, is that *Too Late to Turn Back* shows that however light-hearted a departure is, if the traveller is generous, observant, and dedicated to the trip, the traveller will be changed. From a rather scatty socialite at the beginning, Barbara Greene becomes hardy and courageous without ever being tempted into the role of *memsahib*. How easy it would have been for her to accept the travelling style of the missionary widow of Zorzor, who in Graham's book (where she appears as 'Mrs Croup') 'always travelled in a hammock specially made to carry her weight, with eighteen hammock-carriers. She drove them hard: a ten-hour trek was nothing to her'. Indeed, it is at this very odd woman's house (pet cobra, black baby, Biblical pamphlets) that Barbara reflects:

> I was feeling most extraordinarily well. My feet had nearly healed and were getting beautifully hard. The long walks seemed to suit me, and although the heat was almost too much of a good thing, it now seemed to tire my mind only and not my body. I was getting used to being bitten all over by insects and just went on scratching automatically, thankful that although they bit every other part of my body, they never attacked my face.

Barbara had agreed to go to Liberia because 'It sounded fun'. It wasn't fun. It was almost hell. But after weeks of it, she changed. Habitually she marched behind. Then Graham fell ill, and although he recovered he was still, in her words, 'sub-normal'. 'He looked rather weak, and for the first time I was the one who was marching on ahead'. It is an extraordinary reversal. She had come as a companion, to follow and take orders. But her health was better than Graham's towards the end—her spirits were certainly higher—and on the last lap it was she who set the pace. In the course of this reckless trip, she had grown up and even in a small way taken command. She never says so in the book, just as she never boasts of her good health, but it is clear from what she describes of the last part of the trip. She followed obediently, she nursed Graham through his illness, she made a careful record of the journey. It is no wonder that Graham dedicated his book to her.

Barbara is too modest, too self-effacing, to make any claim for her book. It was not an adventure story, she said. It was not knowledgeable. The reader 'will learn nothing new'. In a delightful aside she says, 'It was the little everyday things that pleased me most'.

One of these things was Graham's presence. How was she to know that in time he would be regarded as one of the greatest English writers? Just as Graham avoids mentioning Barbara in his book, so Barbara never mentions that Graham is a writer, that she has read his books, or that he is making this difficult journey with the intention of writing a book about it. (He had already received, and spent, his advance of £350.) 'I looked up to him', she says, but her role on this trip was every bit as important as Graham's, and just as literary. She is the witness, like the narrator of a novel who sometimes becomes part of the action. She did not know at the time that she was telling a Graham Greene story. In Freetown, Sierra Leone, she took out her diary and analyzed him.

His brain frightened me. It was sharp and clear and cruel. I admired him for being unsentimental, but 'always remember to rely on yourself,' I noted. 'If you are in a sticky place he will be so interested in noting your reactions that he will probably forget to rescue you.' For some reason he had a permanently shaky hand, so I hoped that we would not meet any wild beasts on this trip . . . my cousin would undoubtedly miss anything he aimed at. Physically he did not look strong. He seemed somewhat vague and unpractical . . . Apart from three or four people he was really fond of, I felt that the rest of humanity was to him like a heap of insects that he liked to examine . . . He was always polite. He had a remarkable sense of humour and held few things too sacred to be laughed at. I suppose at that time I had a very conventional little mind, for I remember he was continually tearing down ideas I had always believed in, and I was left to build them up anew. It was stimulating and exciting, and I wrote down that he was the best kind of companion one could have for a trip of this kind. I was learning far more than he realized.

Long after he took the trip, Graham wrote, 'My cousin left all decisions to me and never criticized me when I made the wrong one . . . Towards the end we would lapse into long silences, but they were infinitely preferable to raised voices.'

'Graham', Barbara writes in her book, 'would sometimes become rather obstinate, hanging on to some small, unimportant point like a dog to a bone.' And then she adds, 'But we never quarrelled, not once.'

They had put themselves into a situation in which people nearly always quarrel, or abandon each other, or worse. I once hiked for four days down the same sort of twelve-inch path through tropical jungle. I had three male companions, and at the end of it vowed that I never wanted to see any of them again. The Greenes walked for many days. They succeeded because, as Barbara says in one of her splendid passages, she learned to defer; not to kowtow, but to know when to fall silent. The jungle is not really neutral: it is stubborn and it can drive intruders mad. Barbara discovered conflict-avoidance, though she never uses that pompous phrase. She stayed away from contentious subjects. She said, 'I expect you're right, really'. Soon every subject was contentious, except that of food.

The trip was Graham's idea. Barbara thought of herself as a passenger. But no jungle trek tolerates passengers. Barbara did as she was told, made useful friendships with the carriers, and, following at the end of the long file, observed Graham meticulously. In the beginning, he frightened her a little. She came to respect him, and then to admire him, and towards the end of the trip a kind of understanding was reached. They are like a man and wife in the best marriages, with a profound understanding of each other's strengths and weaknesses; passion is gone, but what has supplanted it—sympathy and trust—is far greater.

Barbara judges Graham not by the way he treats her, but by his manner in dealing with the Africans. Graham did not take any of the advice he was given by the coastal colonials. He had been told to be harsh, to distrust, to shout. Instead, he 'treated them exactly as if they were white men from our own country. He talked to them quite naturally and they liked him'. This got results, 'they did everything he wanted them to do'. And it earned him Barbara's respect. When Barbara remarks, 'he was like a benevolent father', it is like a woman speaking of her husband's love for their children. One must also add that these Africans were being required to venture into a place that was not only strange, but nightmarish: the journey held far greater terrors for them, for they believed in cannibals and devils and people who threw lightning bolts and who could walk through walls and who could kill them with a glance. These Africans had never been on such a trek. They were being led around the back of Liberia and down to the coast. All the paths were new to them, and frightening. It was not only the Greenes who were coming of age as discoverers.

After entering French Guinea, at a very uncertain point in the journey, there is a near mutiny. Graham does not threaten. He is firm; he lectures the men; then he bluffs and turns his back on them. The subtle tactic works better than whips. The men are sheepish; the journey continues. Later, there is a tribal dispute among the men. Graham, who had said, 'There is only one thing to do here—get drunk,' hears the men quarrelling. With the calm and optimism of a little whisky, Graham goes out.

> He listened majestically for a few minutes. Then he gave his verdict firmly, prompted, I suppose, by the faithful Amadu, and lifting up his hand he said, 'Palaver finished.' Then (swaying, oh so slightly) he walked away. It was a superb performance. We were all astonished. The men had no more to say.

A passage that Graham himself chose for comparison with Barbara's book was the one in *Journey Without Maps*, beginning, 'I remember nothing of the trek to Zigi's Town and very little of the succeeding days'. He remembered nothing because he had a high fever, and for several days Barbara thought he was going to die. She kept a close watch on him, what amounted to a vigil, and continued to make notes, which she elaborated in Chapter XII of her own book. The portions of each book are too long to quote here, but a reader would do well to compare them. In any case, the reader of *Too Late to Turn Back* ought also to read

*Journey Without Maps*. Few journeys have been so well recorded, and there are few discrepancies and no contradictions between the two accounts. Because Graham does not mention Barbara very much, he does not say how much the style and shape of her hiking shorts irritated him. Barbara says they drove him nearly to distraction. But his slipping-down socks irritated her quite as much. As time passes, the socks bothered her more and more. It is a measure of her patience that she never mentioned the socks to him. In Monrovia, Barbara says she is going to take her funny shorts back to England ('I could wear them in the country'), and Graham explodes, and 'told me with all the wealth of phrase at his command exactly what I looked like in them. It was worse even than I imagined, and hurriedly and humbly I gave the shorts to Laminah'.

My favourite comparison between the two books concerns the prostitute they encountered in Zigi's Town.

A young girl, an obvious little prostitute, hovered round and postured in front of Graham. She was a beautiful little creature, and I felt that at some time she had been down to the coast and that she had known white men. She was cute and intelligent, but over-optimistic, or she would have realised at once that my cousin was beyond noticing anything.

It is rare, as I said, to have two travel books about the same trip; for the best trips, certainly, one is enough. We have one *Eothen* and one *Arabia Deserta* and one *Waugh in Abyssinia*. In the Greenes we have two Liberias. Graham did most of the leading and arranging, so we know the trip from the head of the column; Barbara mainly followed, she did little arranging, but her book is easy-going and her portraits of incidental characters are warmer and chattier. Graham could be severe, but of course the trip was making him ill. On the night Barbara expected Graham to die, she wrote in her diary, 'Feeling very fit indeed. This weather agrees with me . . .' Graham wrote often about the rats that jumped and played in his hut and prevented him from sleeping—rats are villainous subsidiary characters in his book. Barbara writes, 'The rats were fat and well fed, and apart from the noise they made they left me in peace. For two or three nights they upset me and after that I grew so used to them that I ceased to notice them, and they bothered me no more'.

But what about the prostitute? Barbara had seen her, and she had seen Graham, unshaven, cadaverous, his eyes glazed with fever. He was 'beyond noticing anything'. Or was he? Was the novelist now so sick that he had turned into nothing more than a weary traveller anxious to be free of this dismal setting he had wished upon himself? In Barbara's book he had become at this point a stumbling wreck, fighting towards the coast and fearing the onset of the rains—single-minded, as the sick so often are. There is a parallel passage about the prostitute in *Journey Without Maps*. Graham may have been ill, but he was alert:

> I noted, too, a sign that we were meeting the edge of civilisation pushing up from the Coast. A young girl hung around all day posturing with her thighs and hips, suggestively, like a tart. Naked to the waist, she was conscious of her nakedness; she knew that breasts had a significance to the white man they didn't have to the native. There couldn't be any doubts that she had known whites before.

Graham's glance told him all he needed to know; after all, he had promised his publisher that he would come back with a book. It is the one instance where Barbara guesses wrong about her cousin. In other respects, she is uncommonly sensible, accurate, and perceptive. Graham lives in her book as he does in none other that I know. Barbara had no thought of writing about the trip until her father fell ill; she chose the opportunity to amuse him on his sickbed. She is extremely modest, but her dignity, bravery and loyalty can easily be discerned in these pages. We are very lucky to have this companion-volume, and it is appropriate that no one can read it without reaching the conclusion that Barbara was the best of companions.

June 1981

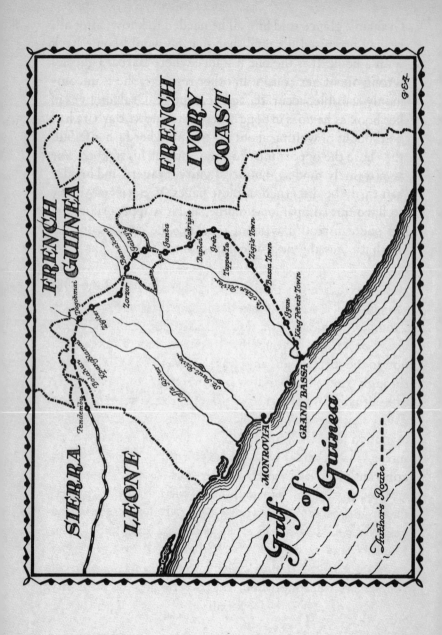

# CHAPTER I

IT all happened after a wedding. "Why don't you come to Liberia with me?" I was asked by my cousin Graham, and, having just had a glass or two of champagne, it seemed a remarkably easy thing to do. I agreed at once. It sounded fun. Liberia, wherever it was, had a jaunty sound about it. Liberia! The more I said it to myself the more I liked it. Life was good and very cheerful. Yes, of course I would go to Liberia. All difficulties vanished in a surprising and slightly disconcerting way. I found out that Liberia was a black republic on the West Coast of Africa. I heard that its rulers were immoral and not to be trusted in any way. I was told that a trek through the hinterland was dangerous and extremely unhealthy. I read that it was one of the few parts of the world that was still unexplored. After a while my sense of elation vanished into thin air. I love my creature comforts; I had no real wish for adventure in the wilds, but apparently it was written in the stars that I should go, and by the time I had found out what I had let myself in for it was too late to turn back. It was all made so easy for me. I was told exactly what to take, and I even found on my arrival in Liberia that I had brought more or less the right things. There were a few mistakes of course. By someone whom I considered a good authority

1

I was told to walk in riding-boots because of snakes. It sounded a little hot and uncomfortable, but who was I to judge of these things? So with a slightly doubtful mind I packed them with my other things. That, however, was but a slight mistake and only worth mentioning as it meant that I had to have shorts made in a great hurry in Freetown at the last minute. These shorts were of strange shape, very full and very brief, that somehow managed to look like a ballet skirt. I am tall and hefty and later, as we got tired towards the end of our trip, these shorts were to get so much on my cousin's nerves that he was ready to scream every time he saw them.

My camping equipment, my food, my ticket, everything was procured for me and I found myself with plenty of leisure to sit back and read *The British Encyclopedia*, the League of Nations Report—which was far from comforting—and any other book or journal about Liberia that I could lay my hands on.

One of the few things that I had to do for myself was to get my visa from the Liberian Consulate in London. This was not so easy as might be thought. As I could not find where the Consulate was from the telephone book, I approached Thos. Cook. After a long wait I was given an address in the City. The numbers in what must surely be the most deserted street in London had apparently all been changed, for the number I was looking for was now a church. It was all very difficult, but I said to myself: "Don't give up. Things will be more difficult than this in the jungle." And so, with new life in me, I eventually managed to track down the Consul in his lair. It was a strange office, small, dirty, and very untidy. A meal was obviously just over, for dirty plates were lying everywhere about the room. The waste-paper basket was full of them. I had brought a friend with me, a Dutchman, and I began to feel glad that I was not alone, for I was not welcomed very warmly. Perhaps I had disturbed their afternoon sleep, or perhaps they were not used to visitors, for they did not seem to know what to do with me. There were two dark young men, and they spoke with a strong accent. "Liberians," I thought. "Pale kinds of half-castes." And if I had not been getting a little tired of sitting there doing nothing I would have got excited at the thought. They could not understand what I wanted, or that one should want to go to Liberia at all. I explained again. I waited. Then one of the young men spoke to the other in another language. To my great astonishment my companion joined in the conversation. They were all Dutchmen. After that we suddenly found ourselves the best of friends. I paid my guinea, and I got my visa, a large red seal stuck into my passport.

After that there was nothing to do except say good-bye. My friends were inclined to be sentimental, for they found it more exciting to believe that I would never return. They had been reading up about Liberia and, rather like myself I am afraid, were inclined to believe in the most lurid reports. So I wept a little, and boasted a lot, and went to a great many farewell parties, and tried very hard to look like an explorer as I left London in a thick mackintosh and a "sensible" hat. And gradually that sinking feeling left me and I was left full of the most glorious excitement. My strength became as the strength of ten. I could have faced a hundred angry tribes, or coped

3

quite easily with a love-sick chief. I went over in my mind all the stories I had heard of Liberia and still, with a child-like *naïveté* believing in them all, imagined myself forever facing danger with a smile.

Now that I am back I can hardly recall all that I was told. Certainly cannibals figured largely, and slavery. Death by the most horrible diseases, and rape, appeared to be such everyday occurrences out there that they seemed hardly worth mentioning. They were just some of the things that one took for granted, more or less. We had been told that there were few wild animals, which certainly eased our anxiety a little bit as neither of us could be called experienced shots. Apart from other things there was also the danger of getting off the track and losing our way. The possibility of starving seemed to me fairly remote. It struck me that we were taking an enormous amount of food. Somehow tins of things look so much more than they really are, as we found to our regret later on.

So we spent our time on board our little cargo boat— named most suitably *The David Livingstone*—thinking of dangers, and learning the jargon of the West Coast of Africa from our five fellow-passengers. We drank "coasters" and ate heavy meals in the stuffy little dining-room. I foolishly slept a great deal instead of, wisely, doing exercises to harden my feet. The days passed slowly but happily. The sunsets were flamboyant as if painted for a second-rate musical comedy, but the nights were warm and starlit, and somehow exciting as only tropical nights can be.

We called at a few ports, but they made little impression

on me. I remember that I had never before seen Madeira in the rain. Then, somewhere else, I remember drinking sweet white wine in the blazing sun, surrounded by glowing bougainvillea. A day or two later I remember the big black eyes fringed by artificial eyelashes, the lumpy figures, and the dirty yellow curls of the Spanish prostitutes in some night club we got to at three o'clock in the morning. The place was filthy. Someone was playing a guitar badly, and someone else was singing shrilly out of tune. A madman, drunk, and with curiously twitching limbs, was walking round the room from table to table, screaming out all kinds of threats.

After a while our excitement grew. There had been an outbreak of yellow fever on the coast and we found port after port closed to us. "Of course," I thought. "The White Man's Grave. That's what they call this part of the world at home. How very pleasant."

We stopped outside the ports. From a distance the little towns looked green and peaceful. At one of these places we left behind us the only other woman passenger, a frightened, repressed little woman who had never before left Liverpool. With a scared face she said good-bye to us and went to join a husband she had not seen since her honeymoon. She was off to start a new life in a continent which she felt in her little provincial soul she would never understand, and where yellow-fever and perhaps death were waiting to give her a welcome.

# CHAPTER II

W E got to Freetown at last.
Graham had never done anything like this before
either. It was, in fact, not at all in his line. Although
cousins, we had never had a great deal to do with one
another before Fate and champagne decided to link up
our lives in this way for three months. I got out my diary
and wrote down what I thought of him. His brain
frightened me. It was sharp and clear and cruel. I
admired him for being unsentimental, but "always
remember to rely on yourself," I noted. "If you are in a
sticky place he will be so interested in noting your reactions
that he will probably forget to rescue you." For some
reason he had a permanently shaky hand, so I hoped
that we would not meet any wild beasts on our trip. I
had never shot anything in my life, and my cousin would
undoubtedly miss anything he aimed at. Physically he
did not look strong. He seemed somewhat vague and
unpractical, and later I was continually astonished at his
efficiency and the care he devoted to every little detail.
Apart from three or four people he was really fond of, I
felt that the rest of humanity was to him like a heap of
insects that he liked to examine, as a scientist might
examine his specimens, coldly and clearly. He was
always polite. He had a remarkable sense of humour

and held few things too sacred to be laughed at. I suppose at that time I had a very conventional little mind, for I remember he was continually tearing down ideas I had always believed in, and I was left to build them up anew. It was stimulating and exciting, and I wrote down that he was the best kind of companion one could have for a trip of this kind. I was learning far more than he realised.

We stayed only a few days at Freetown. We had been given the address of someone out there and had written to him many weeks before, asking him if he would be so kind as to find boys for us who would be willing to go over to Liberia. He wrote back a perfectly charming letter. He would have everything ready for us. He would inform the District Commissioners on the route we would take up-country in Sierra Leone, to expect us. He would be only too delighted to help us in every possible way. When we looked him up soon after our arrival in Freetown we found a most lovable young man. No, he had not yet found us any boys, or told the District Commissioners, or indeed done anything at all. But he would like to help us. Would we care to come to a cocktail party that afternoon? Or what about golf? Or would we like to go bathing?

Once again Fate was to make things easy for us. At the cocktail party there was a certain delightful man, elated enough at that moment to be willing to find boys for two complete strangers, and kind-hearted enough to carry out his promise next day. And no ordinary boys did he find us, but the best in Freetown, and a cook that could not only turn out a four-course dinner in the heart of the jungle out of nothing in particular, but could also manage to look picturesque at all times and in the most trying circumstances. There they stood in a row next morning outside the hotel, in their flowing white robes, their heads bent, their caps held in both hands and pressed against their chests, their eyes lowered. Their dignity overpowered us. Would we ever be able to live up to them? They were completely silent. A little nervously, and in rather literary English my cousin addressed them. By no sign could one see whether they understood or not. They bowed and disappeared. Apparently they accepted the situation, for after that they attached themselves to us. The head boy, Amadu, looked after my cousin. I had Laminah. Amadu never lost his dignity. He was our standard all through our journey. We lacked the courage ever to behave badly in front of the grey-faced little man. Because of Amadu we could not swear if we were angry, I could not cry if I was hurt, we invariably displayed the greatest courtesy towards one another.

Laminah was quite different. I never really learnt to understand what he was saying, but he soon lost his dignity, and chatted and joked all day. He was like a little Cockney street urchin, with a cheeky face and a sense of humour that was of the simplest. On his head he wore a red woollen cap with a bobble, such as one might wear skiing in Switzerland. He was affectionate and lovable, and later, in the depth of the forest, would occasionally decorate my bed with blossoms to prevent my noticing quite so much the dirtiness of the huts.

Amadu and Laminah wore shorts for the trek, but to

the end the cook wore his long trailing white garments. By the time he reached Monrovia scraggy ends floated round him, and he looked like some fantastic scarecrow blowing in the breeze. He was an old man, but cooking was his ruling passion, his life. No matter how long the day's trek had been, how tired and footsore he was, he would come running into the village where we were going to stay the night, usually with a live chicken in his hand. "Where de cook house? Where de cook house?" he would demand from all and sundry, and immediately fall to, happy that at last he was at home in his own surroundings.

While we were in Freetown these three boys hovered round us. Silently they would appear in front of us, with their heads bowed. We felt acutely embarrassed. We knew by this time that they understood us as little as we understood them. They stood and waited. We had no orders to give them while we were at the hotel. What did they want? Always they stood in front of us. Like three ghosts they haunted us. But little by little we became devoted to them. We stayed at one of the two hotels at Freetown. We had heard that it was one of the best along the coast, but this was so hard to believe that we went and had a look at the other one, thinking that we had surely made a mistake and had come to the wrong one. It was perfectly obvious at a glance that no mistake had been made, so we turned back again. There was nothing really wrong with the place at all. It was clean. Later, on our return from Liberia, it seemed the height of luxury. But we had come straight from London, and I suppose we were spoilt. My bedroom had prac-

9

tically no furniture, but what there was had seen much life. I opened the door of my wardrobe and half the inside crashed down. I tried to open the chest of drawers; the handle came out in my hand, but the drawer remained obstinately closed. The paint in the passages had long ago peeled off, so that the walls looked as if they were suffering from some rather nasty disease. I could see outside the windows black, scraggy vultures hopping restlessly in the dust. To my imaginative mind the hotel seemed to have come straight out of a story by Mr. Somerset Maugham. But I felt somehow as if it were cheating me. The stage, so to speak, was all set for a scene of love and murder. Downstairs in the dim evening light the bar looked mysterious. Anything might happen there. Strong, silent men came in and ordered double whiskies and tossed them off. But nothing more did happen. The curtain, I felt, had gone up; the audience was waiting. But the actors had forgotten their lines. We did all the correct things while we were at Freetown. We went to Lumley Beach and admired it. We went to Hill Station where all the white population had migrated and said, how pretty and how nice for the Europeans to live right out of the ugly town like that. We went to a garden party at Government House, chiefly because we had been told that it was amusing to see how all the black guests with one accord dashed at the drinks when they were brought out at 5.30; and we were slightly disconcerted and embarrassed when all the dashing for drinks was done by the Europeans. We made plans and changed them. We bought things we did not want, and we bought other things we would need for our journey, and at the last moment we forgot them and left them at our hotel. I bought my shorts.

We also went to see a very black gentleman who, for some reason that was never very clear, had been banished from Liberia. No one else in Freetown had ever been there. It was a sort of mystery country. One began to wonder if it really existed at all. All kinds of myths and fables had grown up around it. No one wanted to visit this land. Sir James Barrie, had he been with us, would no doubt have been able to write a very pretty little fairy story about it. But as we had come a good long way for that very purpose, it was definitely a country we did want to visit, however mad the people in Freetown told us we were. So we went to call on the Liberian.

We sat in his house a long time getting bitten by insects, and poring over inaccurate maps, and discussing routes and villages very solemnly. Names we never heard of again. Villages we never saw. The English maps of Liberia were so inaccurate that we were told to tear them up and forget them. The American map was even worse, but more dramatic. It had the names of three or four villages marked in the interior, a few dotted lines marking the "probable course of rivers," and was otherwise blank, apart from a few districts marked importantly "jungle," "wild animals" or "cannibals." They were the only maps of Liberia procurable at that time, and we soon realised that they were no earthly good. We must leave things to chance. One always has the feeling that a kind of saint lurks around somewhere to guard the fools of this world. We must make our way somehow from village to village and trust that in the end we would find our way through Liberia. I felt completely placid about the whole thing. I was overcome with the feeling that always afflicts every one acting in amateur dramatics. "It will be all right *On the Night*." One useful thing our black friend did tell us. He spoke of an American Mission at Bolahun, a village that lay just over the border of Liberia. We decided to make for this mission and to stay there for our first night.

The train from Freetown to Pendembu went twice a week, and at last we were ready to go. We got up early that day, and rather self-consciously in my unbecoming shorts I wandered down to the station. Our luggage lay in great heaps on the platform. Beds, tables, chairs, several big wooden cases of food, the water filter, the money-box, two suitcases, and all kinds of odds and ends. Everything that we could think of to keep body and soul together for the next few weeks. A few books: *The Anatomy of Melancholy*, and the stories of Saki and Somerset Maugham. Our boys hovered round. I do not think they had the slightest idea where they were going to. There was much waving and cheering, and the whole of the native population of Freetown seemed to have congregated together for the sheer pleasure of screaming and yelling on the platform. At last we were told that the whistle had blown. We climbed into our carriage and trusted to Providence that the boys had climbed into theirs, and with a roar and a jerk the little train started to wind its way up to Pendenibu.

Pendenibu is as far as the railway runs, 180 miles from Freetown, a journey of two whole days. Two very long days, for the journey was not thrilling. It was hot and dusty, and though we enjoyed the scenery at first for it had the charm of novelty for us, it was not exciting enough to keep our minds from our discomforts. If we opened our windows the dust blew in and got into our food, eyes, hair, noses, and throats so that we spluttered and choked. If we kept them shut we got no air, and the sweat ran down our faces and our shirts stuck to our backs. I looked idly out of the window at the villages we passed by. The natives ran out of their mud huts and waved and screamed at us. To pass the time I tried to imagine what the huts were like inside, for I knew that very soon I would be sleeping night after night in just that kind of place. Probably no worse than this train, I thought. They looked rather picturesque huddled together among the trees in the sunlight.

Up into the hills puffed and panted the little train. Higher and higher. The scenery became more and more uninteresting. Miles of untidy green bush. We could see it stretching over the hills all round us. So we slept and ate very dry sandwiches that the hotel had provided for us at great expense, and tried to read *The Anatomy of Melancholy* and the stories of Saki and Somerset Maugham, till eventually we reached our destination.

The journey must have fuddled my brain because I cannot remember clearly what happened when we got to Pendenibu. My cousin arranged everything. I know we had a long drive along a bumpy road, and arrived at a rest house for the night. After we had washed we walked over to the District Commissioner and drank some warm cocktails with him. I liked him at once, and one of his greatest charms, I thought, was that he had all my cousin's books in a row in his bookshelf. We could not have had a better welcome. While we were talking a white man had slipped silently into the room. He stood quietly by the door and looked startlingly like the usual pictures of Jesus Christ with his carefully cut beard, softly smiling eyes and gentle face. The District Commissioner asked him who he was, and where he had come from. "I would like a bed for the night," said the man with grave dignity, but gave no further explanation. His voice was low and cultured, and he looked strangely aristocratic. The mysterious atmosphere around him pleased Graham, and he asked him to breakfast with us next morning. The stranger accepted.

He came next morning, but we learnt little more about him. He liked the natives, and liked being with them in spite of the impression he gave that he was a little aloof and above everything. I think that that impression was particularly strong, because he was obviously not interested in people like my cousin and myself. He was German, and had spent some years wandering about from village to village, learning old customs, and the various dialects. Very often he would sink into long thoughtful silences, quite forgetful of our presence and quite unembarrassed, thinking deep sad thoughts. He also was going into Liberia, parts of which he knew already. First to Bolahun, and then on. . . . He did not say where to. He was a learner, he said. That was all we found out about him. He was a learner. We saw him to say good-bye to at Bolahun. I would have liked to have asked him so much. He knew so many things, I felt, that I would like to know. He shook my hand, smiled his unamused smile, and walked away into the forest.

We had another lorry drive that took us within four miles of the frontier. From then on we walked. My cousin had hired carriers that would carry our things as far as Bolahun, and there we would have to find others who would come with us through Liberia. The lorry had been late in the morning and our carriers had quarrelled among themselves, which had delayed us. But time no longer mattered; we could leave behind us our European ideas of haste and hustle. It was a lesson that took us some time to learn thoroughly. As if to impress us with this fact all our watches went wrong, and refused to keep time. We put them right whenever we thought of it. "It must be getting very late. It's quite light already. Better put the watches at half-past five," we said to one another morning after morning. Or in the evenings, "I don't think it's too early to have a drink, do you? Let's put our watches at six o'clock."

We arrived at the frontier. Getting our things over the border into Liberia was slow, expensive, but uneventful. We were charged heavily on every single thing we brought in, our revolver (for which we had no licence) being about the only thing to escape detection. It was lying at the bottom of the money-box, where it remained unused for the rest of the trip. We were then told with disarming candour that if they wanted any more money from us they would send a runner to catch us up. The runner turned up all right a few days later and demanded another £6, 10s., which of course we had to pay. After a great deal of delay we eventually got through, and after that we were actually walking in Liberia.

Walking in Liberia. I had come hundreds of miles to do this. And now that I was actually there it seemed rather unreal. Any moment, I thought, I will wake up and find myself in London. I will look out of the window and see the usual damp and dreary January morning. My ancient maid will come in with some tea, and the bath water will probably be cold. I will open the paper and read that Europe is again on the verge of a crisis, that there has been another strike, that unemployment figures are going up, that there have been a few more murders most foul. But surely I was not, I could not, be walking in Liberia. I had done nothing to get there. I had leant back and things had happened to me. The scenery round me, grey and uninteresting, was in the usual monotones of one's dreams. The fact that I was with my cousin whom I really knew so slightly, all added to the mystery. Well, I could at least enjoy it till I woke up.

Graham walked on in front at a most tremendous speed, and I followed at my own pace. It was a habit we started that day and carried on till much later when my cousin fell ill. Then I walked ahead. But in all those weeks we never once walked together. For one thing we would have always wondered if one was keeping the other back, or walking too fast. Also it was too hot. Walking together means talking, or feeling one should talk occasionally. In that heat one needed all one's energy for the sheer physical effort of placing one foot in front of the other for hours on end.

I suppose we left the frontier between one and two in the afternoon, the hottest part of the day. At first we were walking through uninteresting country. There were no trees to give us shade. We stopped very soon for lunch. There were plenty of rocks we could have sat on, but our boys methodically brought out our two chairs and our table. They spread our two tin plates and our knives and forks, and ceremoniously opened a tin of corned beef. We were hungry. Our men ate nothing. They never ate anything during the day, except fruit or colanuts that they picked up by the wayside. We sat by a stream, surrounded by our carriers, who stared at each mouthful we took, each movement we made, while our boys silently waited on us. We were at the edge of the great forest that covers practically the whole of Liberia. We were leaving behind the burnt plants, the long grey grasses, the brown boulders. We were now going to plunge into the greenish half-light of the bush. The boys cleared up. The carriers placed their heavy packs on their heads and on we went. We had not wasted much time over lunch. We thought that by walking hard we could get to Bolahun by five.

The road was rough and very hilly. We scrambled up and down, sometimes on all fours. We did have a hammock with us. I could only use it occasionally, just for five or ten minutes in every hour or two. As we were doing this journey on very little money we did not want to waste too much of it on hammock-bearers. It was the easiest thing to economise on. Also the road was too rough to make much use of it. I liked walking, but it was wonderful to be able to rest my legs every now and then.

It was a strange hammock, with a pole through it to carry it by. Every time we went over a bump the pole crashed down on my nose. Also as it swung a good deal it made one feel a little seasick. Five to ten minutes was quite enough.

At five o'clock we were still striding up hill and down dale at the same tremendous speed. My water-bottle had been empty for some time. "Water," I thought, "just one long drink and I'll be quite happy." Such a modest wish, but I might as well have asked for champagne. There was no water. I should have rationed myself more carefully. It was airless in the forest. I did not notice the trees or the plants. If we went through any villages I did not see them. I wanted a drink and I wanted it very badly indeed.

Little by little the exultation I had felt during the afternoon left me. The way was so much further than we had thought. Hour after hour we walked on. On each side of us there was bush, not as thick as we were to know it later, but thick enough to block out every view. My brain felt woolly. The dream became a nightmare. The sun set and the stars begun to come out. With a last flicker of vitality I found myself highly amused to see that as dusk falls the jungle really does wake up for a short time. Monkeys chattered and swore, birds called, and there was a strange buzzing from a thousand insects, while frogs croaked from every stream. We walked on, tired and footsore, till suddenly we saw our village at the top of a high hill, and utterly tired out I scrambled up the last two miles.

The Fathers of the Mission were at their evening service

when we arrived. I sank down on the steps outside their house and listened to their voices chanting sombrely. Soon they came out to us, welcomed us warmly and took us to the rest-house. Our boys, nearly as tired as we were, unpacked our things and to our great joy discovered a bottle of water. We drank feverishly.

The rest-house was big, with several rooms. The rooms were, of course, completely empty, for all visitors to the mission bring everything they need with them. Our boys before they rested unpacked and made up our beds, draping the long mosquito-nets round them. They put out our wooden table and chairs in one of the rooms they had decided to make our sitting-room. That was as far as we could furnish the house. Even with all my imagination I could not persuade myself that it looked homely. The cook opened a few more tins for our supper, while we drank our quinine.

We sat down to supper silently. We were very, very tired, and while we ate we watched strange insects fly about the room and creep up and down the walls, while the drip, drip, drip of the water in the filter reminded me of the steady monotony of the chorus in a Greek tragedy. Our adventure had begun. Was there any chance of our coming through alive and healthy? Most of our medical supplies had somehow been left behind at Freetown. I had never before known what it was to be quite so weary. Two minutes after I had crept into my hard camp bed, I fell fast asleep.

I woke up refreshed next morning. I lay in bed for a long time before I got up. I had a big whitewashed room, which was quite empty except for my bed and a suit-case. It was very quiet and peaceful. Outside my window I could see an old man sitting on a rock guarding some goats. In the distance a church bell was ringing. It was unmistakably Sunday. A little group of nuns walked up towards the church in their thick black woollen clothes, prayer books in their hands, silent and devout. The sun shed a golden light over everything. The bell stopped ringing. There was no sound now, and a deep peace lay over everything.

I called out to Laminah to bring me a bath. In a few minutes he appeared with the little tin basin we called our bath, and poured three or four inches of tepid water into it. I washed off as much of the dust of yesterday as I could, and put on clean clothes. Then I joined my cousin for breakfast. We had sausages for breakfast. We only possessed a few precious tins of sausages, and had decided to keep them for special occasions. For some reason we agreed that that Sunday morning was a special occasion.

I had a letter of introduction to a gold and diamond prospector. This man, a Dutchman, had made his head-quarters at Bolahun, and we thought that we might get some news of him from the Fathers. So, although wondering whether we would be disturbing them on a Sunday morning, we wandered up to their house. We did not disturb them much, they said, and asked us to come in. They were filling up the time between church and lunch very pleasantly with a game of bridge. The Fathers were full of life and the joy of living; they were natural and without a trace of hypocrisy. And I think they were wise. They lived as comfortably as it was possible to do in that district, had their food sent out from Fortnum and Mason in London, and tried to keep themselves as fit as possible by playing tennis nearly every evening on the rough tennis court they had built for themselves. They told us a little of the work they were doing among the natives. They concentrated a great deal on healing their bodies, for the natives of Liberia suffer a great deal from every kind of disease. We had already seen evidence of this ourselves the day before. Everywhere the natives were walking about with smallpox, yaws, elephantiasis, and covered with venereal sores. A horrible sight, which we saw in every village we stayed at. It was difficult to help them, for they slept huddled together in their dirty huts. The Fathers were trying to teach the village people of Bolahun the elementary rules of hygiene. The children came to the school and learnt that cleanliness is above even godliness. They did not try to stop the native dances, or force the people to wear clothes. As a matter of fact, the natives of West Africa are a vain people, and if they have any money to spend they love to spend it on native cloth to dress up in. The Fathers went their way quietly, healing and teaching, and gradually winning the confidence of the people. There was also a convent of English nuns working in the village. I met them later. The greatest, most human and most lovable teachers of Christianity that it is possible to imagine.

We asked finally about the Dutchman, but he had already gone back to Europe, after only a few months in this country, a sick man, worn out by the climate. But they told us that his partner was living in a tent near our rest-house.

We stopped there on our way home. My cousin looked in. It was hot and stuffy in the tent, and on the bed a man was lying, moaning, and delirious, with a bad attack of fever. All his life he had lived in the tropics, but a few months of Liberia were already getting .him down. We saw him later being carried up to the mission hospital on a stretcher. He was lying quite still, and mumbled incoherently.

After lunch Amadu came and reported himself sick. He was shivering and shaking and was badly frightened. We took him up to the Mission doctor, who dragged him off to the little rough hospital. This meant our staying for a while in Bolahun, for Amadu had already shown himself too precious to be cast lightly aside.

The mission doctor was German, very blond with blue eyes. The first thing one noticed when one entered his house was a large portrait of Hitler, whose stern eyes stared at one accusingly across the room.

"What are you doing wasting time walking across strange countries for no particular reason? Don't you know that life is real, life is earnest?" he seemed to say to me. It quite upset me to see that picture there. It brought Europe too close to one again. All the petty quarrels, and the problems, the rush and the sense of being overpowered by things one hated. It would be good when we got going on our journey and could leave Europe behind at last. I had not expected to find it in Bolahun.

The doctor was young and keen, and had only been out two years. His wife had recently had a baby. She had had it out there, for they were both quite convinced that the climate was healthy if reasonable care was taken. She walked round like a little white ghost. The doctor worked hard and had done wonderful things among the natives. We were sad when we said good-bye to him, for it seemed unlikely that we would ever meet again. We did see him again a few weeks later. We were on our way to England and ran into them both at Freetown in the hotel. His head was bound up and they would not talk to us. Then we heard that, as a result of too much work and the climate, he had gone mad one morning and, imagining something wrong with his throat, had tried to operate on himself in front of a mirror. It was with difficulty that his life was saved.

I spent many hours wandering round Bolahun. It was different from the villages we came across later. The Fathers had transformed it into a kind of Garden City of Liberia, and it even had a slightly provincial atmosphere. The round mud huts were freshly whitewashed, and their palm-thatched roofs were neat and tidy. They were nearly all surrounded by prim little gardens. The streets were broad and clean. But it was beautiful. Everywhere the cotton flowers were blooming, yellow and pink, and an enormous tree, covered with rose-coloured blossoms, towered above the village, adding a beautiful tinge of colour against the pure deep blue of the sky. Growing rice and cotton were the chief industries of the village, as in all the places we passed through. The needs of the natives are very simple, a handful of rice to eat every day, a hut which they share with their whole family, and a little strip of cloth to wear. Their only problem is to raise somehow five shillings a year for their hut tax. But they were happy and contented. The women sat in the sun playing with their babies. I never saw a child cry except with fright when it saw my cousin or myself. Nerves and ill-temper were things that belonged to the rush of Europe. Here a natural sense of courtesy and hospitality were the chief characteristics of all the village people that we met.

Bolahun is also a market town, and every now and then, on market days, villagers would come for miles around and meet a little way out of the village with their wares. I went down to see it. The crush and smell was overpowering, and the sight of all the diseased bodies rather upset me. I bought a rug and some silver ornaments. Then I saw our cook buying strange foods for our supper, and I hurried away, preferring not to see it in its natural state. The sooner I learnt to eat without wondering what I was eating the better. Whatever it was the cook produced that night, it was very good. Much, much later when we were getting short of food I rebelled for the one and only time. Our boys suggested that we should try a little monkey, but I had just seen it lying about, and it looked too much like a shrivelled, dried-up black baby. I could not face it.

We needed a boy while Amadu was ill, so the Fathers sent us Mark, who was still a school-boy at their school. He was shy and awkward as any English school-boy of about fourteen, but he had a sense of humour and a strong feeling for any dramatic situation. He would love to slip into our rest-house quite silently in the darkness of the evening and stand still in a corner. He would not

24

move for a long time, so that we would forget he was there, and then suddenly he would make a noise. When we looked round startled he would giggle and run away. He was a Christian and proud of it, and loved to tell us of his lessons. One day he asked if King George of England was still alive. We assured him that he was and asked what he had learnt about him at school. "Plenty. Plenty," he replied. "I can't tell you. Also about the Priz of Whiz."

We soon realised that above all things in the world Mark wanted to trek with us down to Monrovia. Already in his imagination he was telling the other school-boys about it. He would be a hero for weeks on his return. One morning we received the following letter from him:

"SIR,
    In honour to ask you that I am willingly to go with you to Monrovia please kindly I beg you and Miss or Madam.
    Because you love me so dearly. I don't want you must leave me again. And moreover I am too little to carry a load. I will be assisting the hammock until we reach. Me and the headman. Please sir, dont leave me here again. I was fearing to tell you last night. Please Master, good Master, and good servant.
                                        Yours ever friend,
                                                    MARK."

We decided to take Mark, soothing our consciences over the extra expense by telling ourselves that he would be useful as an interpreter for he could speak several dialects. Our boys, of course, could not speak any of the Liberian tribal languages, and our carriers later could hardly speak any English. Mark, however, became even more important as a kind of court jester, for he was always ready to joke and play the fool when spirits got low. Like any schoolboy in the world he was thrilled with anything unusual that turned up. We never regretted taking Mark with us.

In the evening we were entertained with music. We had two native harps made for us, and one of the natives would come and give me lessons. Though the notes were easy and the same bar would be repeated sixty or seventy times on end, the rhythm was beyond me. It was so strange to my ears, that I could not even hear what I was doing wrong. I never progressed very far. We had the added difficulty of never being able to converse except in signs and smiles. But after the lesson the harpist would sit in a corner of the veranda staring dreamily at the hurricane lamps and play hour after hour. He was a member of the Buzie tribe, which is supposed to be the only artistic tribe in Liberia. He had a sensitive face and never stopped playing for a moment, till one felt as if his body had gone away and only his spirit remained. The instrument had a pretty tinkling sound, rather like a child's musical-box, and gradually out of the shadows dark figures would draw near and start dancing. One man after another would join in quietly. Their arms would hang limply at their sides, and their heads drooped down. They would shuffle round and round the veranda with small steps, hardly lifting their feet from the ground. It was rather a dismal performance. Only one little boy of about ten years old would show more spirit. He darted about, every movement full of grace, bending down covering his face one moment, and then stretching up to his full height the next. The dreary men behind him, shuffling about, took no notice of him. The boy's dancing was dramatic, and was the only dancing in Liberia where I almost understood what the performer was trying to express.

The days slipped by. Amadu was still ill, but we did not mind very much. I wanted the time to go slowly. I wanted to remember every moment, every spot. Also it was very comfortable at Bolahun, and I could not help wondering what we were going in to. I began at last to feel Europe slipping into the background. To lose my feeling for time. The hours, the days, glided into one another. I began to like the heavy, sweet smells of Africa. I liked eating rice at every meal. I loved to walk round the villages at night, to peep inside the huts and see the natives huddled together round the open fire. Most of the huts had one round room. The fire in the middle helped to keep the insects out. Also here in Bolahun they needed the fire at night for warmth, for being so high up in the hills it got cold at night, although it was so hot in the daytime. I even got used to our primitive lavatory in a tin shed near our rest-house, the seat crawling with ants. It was not long before I began to look back on it as a luxury that I had not properly appreciated at the time.

One day we walked over to the next village. The chief had died, and we had heard the tom-tom beating in the distance. After the death of a chief the village always celebrates the third, the seventh, and the fortieth days with dancing and feasting. On our arrival we were welcomed by the new chief in the usual way by clasping hands and gently withdrawing them and clicking the fingers at the end. The chief took us into a very stuffy hut and entertained us with the music of drums and rattles. In the midday heat we felt as if someone was beating us on our heads. I could see little insects hopping about on my bare knees, but they jumped away under my clothes when I tried to catch them. Rattle, rattle, rattle. Bang, bang, bang went the music. Nothing but noise and rhythm, while more and more people crowded into the hut to stare at us. There were no insects hopping about on Graham, and he did not seem to want to scratch his arms and legs and back as I was doing by this time. I thought it rather heartless of him to be so immune when I was in such agony, so I pointed out my knees to him, which were coming up in red inflamed bumps. He smiled sympathetically but wearily. He was feeling the heat and stuffiness of the hut more than I was, so I felt we were even.

A man with a big drum arrived and several women with more rattles. More noise. Every one started swaying and stamping their feet. I began to feel the excitement myself, and forgot my bites for a few moments. But it went on and on. There was no climax. It just went on and there seemed to be no reason why it should ever stop.

But at last quite suddenly the chief called for the devil to dance for us. We got out of the stuffy hut and stood outside. At that time we were still ignorant of the true significance of the West African devil, but we enjoyed its strange appearance and the energetic way in which it danced. It had on long flowing skirts of raffia, a feathered head-dress, and a weird mask with a kind of beak which it could open and shut by pulling a string. He ran up and down in the dust, swaying and bowing to right and left. After about twenty minutes he stopped, and we got away and walked through the village. We saw a large pit in which were seated all the widows of the dead chief. They each had on a minute pair of drawers, and were covered hair and all from head to foot in grey clay. All day they were to sit there, while the youngest mother sat on the grave of the chief nearby. She had on a native cloth and was not covered with clay. Next day they would all be washed, their bodies would be oiled and they would be passed on to the next chief.

The marriage laws of the hinterland of Liberia are very simple. A man may have as many wives as he can pay for. A really good young virgin costs anything between £10 and £20, but of course there are many that can be bought very cheaply indeed. One chief we met had 230 wives, but he was old, and they were cheating him now by selling some of his wives to him over and over again, for he was too blind to notice the difference. If a man had a great many wives he cannot spend a great deal of time with each one, and in that case a wife can find for herself a lover. Unless the wife tries to hide the lover the practice is not discouraged; in fact, it might almost be said to be encouraged, for the husband is entitled to collect a certain sum of money from each lover who so provides him with a steady income. Moreover, all the children belong to the husband and they look after him in his old age. If the wife is unhappy, she may go back to her family, who then have to pay back the money they received for her on her marriage. It is all very simple and complications cannot, I imagine, often arise. There seems to be no jealousy among the wives, and each new one is welcomed into the family circle on the grounds that many hands make light work. They certainly seemed to be very contented as they were sitting together, pounding rice, feeding their babies, and delousing each other's hair.

# CHAPTER III

THE time came at last for us to leave Bolahun. Amadu had left the hospital and had quite recovered his health. He was cheerful enough to come and borrow some money from his wages to buy himself "fine country clothes," a kind of loose garment made in blue and white stripes. The Fathers had found us twenty-six carriers who would come with us all the way to the coast, to Monrovia, the capital of Liberia, and they helped us to plan a route through the lesser known parts of the country. This was no easy matter for, as the maps were of no use, they could only give us the direction and the names of one or two villages to aim at. It was the best we could do, and we started off anyway in the direction they suggested. We were hopeless amateurs. We had neither of us been to Africa before. We knew nothing. Our boys from Freetown, and Mark, could speak a strange kind of English, which after a while we learnt to understand to a certain degree, but with our carriers we could never hold any kind of conversation. Practically the only English words that they knew were "too far." We would suggest going on to the next village. "Too far, too far," they would yell and sit down firmly on the ground. This was their most exasperating trick. Nearly always they said it from sheer laziness, but just occasionally when we insisted on going on they would prove to be right. Mark was our interpreter, but when he grew excited his voice rose to a scream and a giggle and he would be covered with shyness; so that at really critical moments he would be quite useless.

We set off one morning with a light heart. A long, long line of us winding down the road. Our carriers were a strange crew. The headman was always very smart, with his shirt hanging outside his trousers. As a head man he was not very efficient, being completely incapable of organising anything, but he was good-natured and the men liked him. The others were ragged, most of them naked except for their loin cloth. The sweat streamed down their backs. They carried their heavy packs on their heads, and worked hard for their three shillings a week.

They were to be paid at the end of the journey, for we did not want to run any risk of being deserted suddenly, but they were allowed to borrow 3d. or 6d. occasionally. Some of them were lazy and all exasperating at times, but we grew very fond of them. They brought us their silly little quarrels to settle when we were tired. They smelt horribly; they chewed cola-nuts they picked up from the ground as they walked along. But they were child-like creatures, easily amused, living in the moment, and at the beginning of the trip before we got overtired they would suddenly burst into song as they ran along on their thin little legs. Strange, monotonous songs. One man would start and the others would join in, singing the same thing over and over again. I asked Mark what they were singing, and he explained that they sang before they came to a village to tell the villagers who we were, and all they knew about us—he would not say what that was—and telling them they need not be afraid of two white-skinned people. They were extraordinarily honest; although we left our possessions lying scattered about the huts we occupied, we never missed the smallest article. They tried to beg and wheedle them out of us at the end, but they never stole. We had enough money in our money-box to have kept them all in luxury for many a long day, but we realised at once that the idea of running off with it would never enter their heads.

After walking for about two hours we arrived at Kulahun, the home of the District Commissioner. We owed him £2 each for our permits of residence that every visitor to Liberia must pay. It was overdue, and we decided to call on him and pay it. As usual we were in luck. The President of Liberia was staying there and sent a message that he would like to see us.

We had already heard of Mr. Reeves, the District Commissioner. He was very much feared in that territory. He was a Mohammedan, a fat flabby figure in bright and gaudy clothes, and a red fez over his black greasy face. It was a cruel and sensual face. One heard all kinds of stories about him. Rumours grow, of course, but we had heard from Mark that burning natives alive in their huts was a form of punishment his ingenious brain had thought out. He used unpaid labour for any work that he wanted carried out, and overseers stood over these men with long whips to make them work harder. He was loathed and feared. He was a relative of the President's, and so it was believed that he would never be removed. The rumours had become so persistent that Monrovia was forced to take notice of them, and the President himself had come to listen to the complaints of the chiefs. The President came. But by the time he arrived the chiefs had been bribed and threatened and had no complaints to make. Mr. Reeves stayed on.

While we were waiting for the President, we were entertained by one of his A.D.C.'s, a suave, polite young man, smartly dressed in a brown-coloured uniform, not unlike that of a Nazi storm-trooper. We sat down rather gingerly, as if we were at a suburban tea-party, and the A.D.C. made a few remarks about the weather. "Very hot for the time of year, is it not?"

"Yes. I expect the storms will be breaking soon."

"Quite. Rather dusty, is it not?"

"Yes, indeed," we answered, thinking of our unprepossessing appearances. After that the conversation rather died out, and we sat round in solemn speechlessness while he played a record on the gramophone. *J'ai deux amours*, sang Miss Josephine Baker over and over again.

A beautiful black girl, dressed in European clothes, entered and sat quietly in a corner. She never spoke a word, but shuffling a pack of cards in her hands watched us languidly. She was plump and had black dreamy eyes, and immediately brought to one's mind the stories of the Thousand and One Nights. She was one of the President's "most intimate friends," we were told afterwards, and he had recently made her father a Judge of the Supreme Court.

The atmosphere changed. The President hurried in, looking as if he had just left the Fifty Shilling Tailors, and the room was filled with his enormous vitality and spirit. He was jovial, he was restless. He laughed his big fat laugh, and then he became wistful, even sad, sentimental, serious, and then in a flash back again to the height of good humour. He was like a successful actor showing off his whole bag of tricks. But he was a brave man. There were the Presidential elections coming on soon and he was doing what no President of Liberia had ever done before—a tour in the country. The last President had once travelled from Sierra Leone to Monrovia with 200 soldiers to protect him, but this man was doing a real trip of the hinterland with a guard of only thirty men. He travelled quickly, of course, and the natives were now unarmed; but they still had their swords and their primitive weapons. He boasted about his popularity almost as if he really believed in it.

The constitution of Liberia is based on that of America. Nearly a hundred years ago when the slaves of America gained their freedom a good many of them were sent over to Liberia, for it was difficult to know what on earth to do with them all. Liberia was then completely primitive and was uninhabited except for the native tribes living in the bush. The American slaves settled and became the rulers of Liberia, taking English names or adopting the names of their former masters. The descendants of those slaves are now the upper class and the governors of Liberia, and still speak English with a strong American accent.

My cousin asked the President if his position in Liberia was the same as that of the President of America. He replied, almost hurt at the question, that his authority went much further.

"Once elected and in charge of the machine, I'm boss of the whole show."

He had been President for the last four years, and was hoping to get re-elected. He told us of all the work he had been doing during his last term of office. The roads he had started, which he hoped would be ready for motor traffic in a few years time. He even talked vaguely of aeroplanes in the near future. When we finally got to Monrovia, we found it full of evidence of his ideas. Roads that had been started and that had never been, and would never be, finished. Houses half-built, planned on the most ambitious scale, that were now falling into ruins. His ideas were splendid, but he had too many. Before one was finished the next one was started and interest in the first had already waned.

I liked the President. He was not wily or crafty. He did things, one felt, in a big way. If he was up to any tricks he would be dishonest in the grand style, rather splendid. I was sorry when after an hour we had to shake him by his big black hand and wish him good-bye.

We went out again into the sunlight, and marched on. It was a walk of incredible beauty. In spite of the heat, which in a few moments made my shirt lie wringing wet against my skin, and my hair lie damp against my cheek, my mind was fresh. I noticed everything, and each picture was imprinted vividly in my memory. Little streams we had to cross were covered with butterflies of every shade, that rose in a cloud and fluttered round us as we passed by; strange plants in the undergrowth; little gleaming pink flowers everywhere; the strange, weird shapes of the towering trees with their long hanging foliage. The long black armies of ants, winding their way through the forest. If one had the misfortune to step too near them they would rise up and fasten themselves with their sharp little claws on to one's skin. It was impossible to pull them all off oneself, and there was nothing to be done except to call one's boy and he would drag them off one by one, which was a slow and rather painful performance.

High up above us the monkeys leapt lightly from branch to branch, like trapeze artistes, twirling and revolving, and jumping incredible distances, as if they wanted to show off their best tricks to us.

Every now and then I would hear a slight rustle, and a snake would glide off into the undergrowth near me. Strange black birds, whose wings as they flapped made a weird scraping noise which echoed through the forest, flew round our caravan. I can still remember the delicious taste of the warm boiled water in the water-bottle. It was a wonderful and exciting trek. Everything was still new, and thrilled me. It was amusing to be carried over the streams on the back of one of the hot smelly carriers, knowing that I must not let the cool-looking water touch my skin. The stream that was looking so appetising was treacherous. It was swarming with little guinea worms; nasty creatures that could force their way under one's skin through any little sore or scratch. If one of these creatures managed to establish itself happily, it would start to grow and gradually elongate itself right up the veins of the leg, and the only way to remove it would be to find the end, and carefully, without breaking it, pull it out by rolling it round a match. We were not fussy about most things, but this operation did not appeal to me and I decided to be careful.

I was exhilarated by the fun and novelty of everything. I still had that champagne feeling with which I had entered this adventure. It was only very gradually that I saw that it was more than fun, when I began to see the beauty of this strange land: the women rhythmically pounding the rice; the naked babies playing in the dust; the little villages with their mud huts painted white and thatched with palm leaves, set high on a hill like some mediaeval fortress; the magical moonlight nights, and weird music.

But that first day it was sheer fun. It was not a long walk, and it was afternoon when we reached the village where we wanted to stay the night. The influence of the American Mission could still be felt very strongly here. The chief's son had been to the school and could speak English. It was a clean village and a busy one.

As I drew near I began to feel ill. I had such a pain that I could hardly walk the last half-mile. I was scared. Had I caught some disease already? I had been in contact with so many sick people. I was enjoying myself so much, and I simply could not bear the idea that perhaps it was finishing already. We had not as yet completely escaped from the greedy, outstretched hand of civilisation. I must not get ill now. First of all I must see what Nature, unspoilt and untouched, was like, for I had come a long way and did not want to be cheated at the last moment from comparing it to the civilisation I had always known of London and Paris. I had always liked contrasts, and I hoped that I would not be done out of examining the sharpest contrast I had ever known. A prayer came to my mind that I had not thought of since the days when I used to be sick at children's parties. "Please God. Don't let me be ill just yet. Not just yet." I tottered into the village and saw Graham in the same state.

"Hell," I thought. "We *have* caught something."

I longed to wash the dust off my face and to lie down, but our social duties prevented me. The chief welcomed us, using his son as interpreter. He was a hospitable man and proud of his village. We were taken for a tour of inspection. Like visiting royalty, in a kind of night-mare, we were shown the smithy, the preparation of the cotton in all its stages, the dyeing. And finally the devil danced for us. He had a fine mask, rather cruel in ex-pression, and long raffia skirts. Up and down he danced, up and down, asking for more and more money, which we, poor innocents that we were, handed over to him. Apart from my pains my feet had blistered, and each step that I took brought tears to my eyes.

At last it was over. The chief showed us our hut, which was big, with two rooms, and we were given time to wash. Every drop of water had to be boiled, but that little basinful, though it could not possibly have cleansed us, refreshed us. I bathed my bleeding feet and put on my big, soft, comfortable mosquito boots. Feeling better, we sat outside the hut and sipped whisky to revive our-selves. We had hardly sat down when the chief returned with many presents for us. This time we were given a goat, rice, palm wine, about sixty oranges, some stringy chickens, and a basketful of bad eggs. It was a custom of the country to give back in presents the same amount as one had received. They preferred it mostly in money, to enable them to pay their taxes, but we had brought presents, of course, with us as well. We had been told in England that the world had grown so sophisticated that presents from Woolworths were no longer good enough. So we had tried to be original. We had bought many knives, which were, of course, completely useless for they made far better ones themselves. We had also bought a quantity of "housewives," filled very neatly with coloured threads, and needles of all sizes. We were very proud of these and decided to keep them till we got to the really primitive parts. We were quite sure that the natives would be thrilled. As we approached the primitive districts it gradually dawned on us that the natives there would have nothing that they could possibly sew. It was one of those mistakes that one cannot understand afterwards ever having made. All our beautiful "housewives" came back with us.

Our boys started bringing out our supper, and as soon as I saw it I realised what was wrong with us. Our cook had baked bread the day before, and as we had no yeast he said he would make it with palm wine instead. The experiment had been a complete failure. The result was disastrous, but I felt overjoyed when I realised it was nothing more serious.

But supper was out of the question for me. There was nothing to be done except retire to bed before the chief could catch us again with some more entertainments. It was my first experience of sleeping in a native hut, but it was clean, and, anyway, I was far too tired to care about anything. As I dropped off to sleep I could hear the sweet tinkling of the native harp outside my hut, and the sound of continuous laughter.

Next morning we got up soon after five feeling much better, though my feet felt far worse. But there was nothing to be done about that except pretend that it did not matter. Nothing in the world would have made me confess what they really felt like. Some of the jibes and jeers that had been directed against me, when I had first announced my intention of walking through Liberia, were still too fresh in my mind. "We can just imagine Barbara tripping through the jungle in her high-heeled shoes!" Well, there I was, and my feet were glowing hot and sore. I was angry about it, for it took my mind off more important things for the next few days.

The chief came back with more presents. He brought us a monkey which amused our boys, and which made its home on Mark's head till we lost him a few weeks later. Laminah behaved appallingly badly towards the monkey. Till the joke wore thin, he would tease and torment the wretched animal, poking it with sticks, slapping it, throwing it about, dragging it by its string through the dust, while the creature hissed and snapped at him. For a few days it was a never-ending joke and delight to him. Later he got rather fond of it, and would give it little bits of food. The chief also gave us another chicken, three knives, a little red-leather bag, and a request that we would send him a hat from England.

We were a strange caravan when we finally left the village at eight o'clock, with our four boys and twenty-six carriers, the goat and the monkey and five live chickens. Our cook brought up the rear in his flowing white robes, carrying an open knife in his hand. Our loads were added to presently, for we met a black missionary who took us into his hut and presented us with sixty unripe bananas, and also, no doubt unconsciously, all kinds of fleas and bugs.

It was a walk like the day before. I began to wish we could see a little more. The track was merely a rough passage through the bush that the natives had cut between village and village. It was very narrow and we walked in long Indian file. Most of the time one had to look down on the ground, for the roots of the trees and the long foliage would trip one up. The forest closed in on us on both sides, thick and impenetrable. The monotony of walking through the dense forest without views, without sunlight, or change, had not yet begun to bore us. That was to come later. At the moment I enjoyed scrambling along up and down the rough paths, trying to keep fairly close to Graham, who walked on so fast ahead.

We had one short rest for lunch, but all the rest of the day we walked on steadily and rapidly. I was away from Europe and all those things we call civilisation at last. War could break out and I would not hear about it for weeks. We could die and no one would find us. No letters could reach us. No one in the world had the slightest idea where we were. For at least a month we would hear nothing of the outside world, of our friends or our relatives. All of which gave me a childish feeling of satisfaction. I felt I was accomplishing something, though I actually knew quite well that I was accomplishing no more than if I were sitting in an arm-chair at home. I felt rather ashamed of myself for feeling excited at the thought that we would presently be walking through parts of the world that white people had probably not walked through before. I was truly ashamed at such a futile thought, but all the same I could not help being thrilled. I knew perfectly well that my journey through Liberia would bring no benefit whatsoever to humanity, and that certainly we would contribute nothing new to the scientific world. We were even incapable of describing the birds and plants that we saw, and had no idea if they were really rare or strange. But it was like reading thrilling adventure stories in one's early school-days, when invariably one identified oneself with the hero. "Slipping silently through the jungle he felt a million unseen eyes watching him. Clasping his gun in his hand he stood still and held his breath. Was that a lion he heard roaring behind him?" And so on, page after page. The fact that I had no sensation of a million watching eyes, and that there were no roaring lions anywhere near me, did nothing to suppress my excitement. After all, I quite honestly did not know what I would come across. I did not expect to see a lion, but if one should cross my path, I did not even possess a gun to clasp in my hand.

At this point I must pause and deliver one word of warning. Should the reader of this book lean towards the roaring lion type of adventure, let him cast this volume from him. The beasts of the forest kept away from us, the natives were friendly, our adventures were more amusing than frightening, and good luck dogged our footsteps most of the time. The old type of Adventure in the Wilds seems to have disappeared.

It is hard to say what has become of it. Perhaps we have all become too prosaic, too unimaginative. Things no longer seem to happen to us as they did to explorers of old. Yet I feel convinced that the old writers were truthful. Perhaps it is we who have lost their spirit; we no longer see the adventurous. We cock an amused eye and wait for the next thing to turn up. The cinema has taken away so much that was mysterious. However excited I felt, however happy, so much of what I saw was in some vague way familiar, seen a hundred times in travel films and in geographical magazines. Nowadays if we want hair-breadth escapes we must turn again to the school-boy stories, written by men who have probably lived all their lives comfortably in England.

Or should the reader have a keen, searching mind and hope to gain great knowledge from this book, let him, too, cast it from him. He will learn nothing new. I confess now that I who undertook this trip so impulsively, returned to England with a deep love in my heart for the beauty of the primitive villages, but remained appallingly ignorant to the end of the wild, untouched nature around me. I was also more interested always in the natives than in the politics of an adolescent government. It was the little everyday things that pleased me most.

We walked on and on. After a good many hours it became obvious that we were right off the track. My cousin, with praiseworthy optimism, called out from time to time that we had only another two hours' walk, but as hour after hour passed I was forced to believe that he was under some delusion on the subject. Once again we were walking after the sun had gone down and the stars were peeping out. The path was very rough and hilly, and we had been walking hard since eight o'clock in the morning. Each hour now seemed like a long lifetime. Once again I had not been very clever at rationing myself over my water-bottle. My feet were more sore than ever, and every step I took was the most exquisite agony. We came to a broad river which we had to cross by hammock bridge. This was not very easy in the dark. The bridge was made of pieces of wood, bound together by fibre, and hung on to the high trees on each side of the river. The bridge swayed as we crossed, and our weariness made us stumble.

After about another hour we reached a village at last. Even in the dark we could see it was filthy, and that it was not good, honest dirt, but something that had turned foul and bad. Disgusting, diseased men and women sat round and stared at us. No white people had ever stayed there before. I sat down somewhere and took off my shoes. My feet were bleeding. But for Graham the real work of the day began. By means of interpreters who could not understand one another, he had to find huts, and food for the men. This was a long and irritating business, and the only thing on our trip that caused me continual astonishment every day to the end was the way my cousin managed to do this always with unfailing patience.

At last huts were found for us, and I was glad that it was too dark to see clearly the families who moved out to make room for us. The boys swept out the place a little bit, but it was late and they were tired, and it was

45

only possible to get out the worst of the filth. We could see how weary the boys were, for Amadu suddenly lost control of his nerves and seizing a stick he beat and struck with all his strength some of the carriers who got in his way. Surprisingly they did not mind, but laughed good-humouredly and moved away. There was some rumour that the carriers with our beds had been unable to get over the bridge. A night in that village without mosquito-nets would undoubtedly have brought us down with fever, so we were not a little relieved when they turned up.

I sank down on my bed too tired to eat, too tired to undress, too tired even to wash. We must have walked nearly thirty miles in that heat, and along those rough tracks. I thought I would go to sleep at once. I blew out my light.

Immediately there was a scampering and a scratching, and with a rush an army of rats tore down the walls. I could see their black shadows, and I could hear them scuffling round the room. Overhead I could make out the dim shadows of the bats flying about, and the mosquito-net was powerless to keep out the fleas and bugs. I put my hand gingerly out of my net, caught hold of a shoe and threw it at a great mass of rats. They hardly noticed. I lit my hurricane lamp, but this did not disturb them at all, so I blew it out again, for I preferred not to see them. I sat up in bed. I was bitten all over in a few moments, and my feet burned. The monkey was tied up all night outside the hut and scratched restlessly on the wall. In the early morning the beasts of the village tried to make their way through the door. All night the rats played their noisy games round my bed.

# CHAPTER IV

BY five o'clock the village was astir. The darkness
gradually changed into a misty grey light, and the
rats scuttled away into their hiding-places. The night
had seemed endless. Although I had always been told
that the rat population of London was as great as the
human population, I had never before seen one in my
life. They are dirty creatures, and though no doubt
there have been times when a tamed rat has been a
solace and a joy to some poor prisoner shut away and
forgotten for life, it is not an animal one would befriend
from choice. My disgust of rats had been strengthened
perhaps on the voyage out, for I had been reading *Four
Frightened People* during the long days on board. The
story came back to my mind vividly as I sat up in bed.
There is a realistic description of a rat running along a
passage. Suddenly it tumbles over and lies quite still.
It is dead. The dreadful realisation gradually awakes in
the mind of the onlooker that bubonic plague has broken
out on board.

I had read in the British Government Blue Book a
list of diseases that flourish in the interior of Liberia.
I went over them in my mind. Malaria, elephantiasis,
yaws, hook-worm, smallpox, dysentery. Did it also
mention plague? I racked my brains and tried to see the

print before my eyes. I remembered the rats of Monrovia were mentioned. Yes. And, of course, it also said that no steps were taken against plague, that nothing was organised to prevent it spreading and that there was no medical supervision whatsoever of boats touching the Liberian coast. I listened to the rats rushing round my hut, and remembered that plague is carried by rats.

I spent the whole night sitting up in bed frankly terrified. My hands moved round the edge of my bed, continuously tucking in my mosquito-net. I had a fearful idea that if the rats were hungry they might bite through the net, and start nibbling my toes. One of the nuns at Bolahun had most vividly described to us how she had woken up one night to find a rat on her face. A singularly unpleasant experience. In the darkness of the night my imagination ran riot. I wondered how many there were round me. But I need not have been so scared. The rats were fat and well fed, and apart from the noise they made, they left me in peace. For two or three nights they upset me and after that I grew so used to them that I ceased to notice them, and they bothered me no more.

It is strange, and perhaps rather horrible, how quickly we adapt ourselves to our surroundings. My life in England had been laid in pleasant places. All my life I had been used to well-cooked food and beautiful clothes, a lovely house filled with people who smoothed out for me as far as possible the rough patches on my road through life. I was taken care of and spoilt both by my family and my friends, and the little, dull, tiresome everyday household things were automatically done for me. I had liked to find my evening clothes spread out for me ready pressed on my bed, my bath ready for me, and then to come down to a dinner lit by candle-light. Beauty, comfort, and a good deal of luxury had been part of my life. I was used to it, and I knew that when I returned to England it would immediately become part of my life again. In Liberia I was surrounded by rats, disease, dirt, and foul smells, and yet in a very few days I had sunk to that level and did not mind at all.

We never had enough boiled water to wash really properly. Our clothes were never clean. The bristles of my hair-brush were eaten away entirely by the rats in this dirty village. It was my own fault, for I had left the brush out of my suit-case, but it meant that there was nothing I could do except throw it away; and so for the next two months—till I reached England—I did not brush my hair again. It got stiff with dust and stood out round my head like a halo. Graham looked rather unshaved. It was not long before he gave up all attempt at shaving and tried to grow a beard. It did not get along very fast, and he never really passed the untidy beach-comber stage. My face was burnt and brown, and the dust was so rubbed into it that it took me literally weeks when I got to England to get it to look normal again. I kept my nails short, but they got broken round the edges. I was quite certainly not a thing of beauty, a joy for ever. But it did not worry me. It was all part of the existence we were leading and seemed to be perfectly natural.

We dressed, and while I was dressing I tried to see where the swarm of rats could now be hiding. But they were completely invisible. It was necessary to be careful not to put one's foot on the ground unless one had very thick soles to one's shoes. Nasty little jiggers would worm their way under one's toe-nails and happily make their home there. Though it was quite easy to have them cut out, and not particularly painful, it became tiresome if one did not notice it at once and started off on the day's trek, for the jigger would grow and send little pin-pricks of burning pain through one's foot. But however careful we were, they would creep into our feet somehow, and we soon got used to calling for the boy to come and cut them out.

I went out into the sunlight. The village was even dirtier than we had realised the night before. The tumbled-down huts were huddled together, so that there was hardly any space between them. The whitewash round the base had long ago peeled off, so that they looked grey and down-at-heel. A hideous woman walked round scraping up goat dung with her hands, on one of which there was an open sore. Goats, cows with their ribs sticking up under their thin flesh in unsightly lumps, chickens and unhealthy dogs were wandering around. The smell was sickening, and as there was a slight breeze the filthy dust blew into our eyes and throats.

Our carriers were making no attempt to get our things packed up. They were sitting about in the dust languidly and lazily. During the night they had spread themselves through the village, sleeping in whichever hut had room for extra inhabitants, for even in this village the spirit of hospitality was very great. The headman was walking about in his usual dreamy fashion. In his right hand he carried a rattle that he always had with him, and which he would shake rhythmically. He walked among the men, smiling his pleasant, vague smile, good-natured, charming, and utterly inefficient.

The name of the village was Duogobmai, and my cousin asked how far it was to Nicoboozu, which was one of the villages we were aiming at. The cry we were to hear so many times throughout our journey from our carriers rose up to heaven firmly and loudly that morning. "Too far. Too far."

"We can't stay here," we said. "It's disgusting. How far is it to the next village?"

"Too far. Too far." And the carriers sat firmly on the ground and refused to budge.

We could not blame them. The trek the day before had been very hard, and we knew that they deserved a rest. Amadu's feet were sore, and though they healed much faster, that morning they looked nearly as bad as mine. But he did not complain. The boys had been told in Freetown to look after us and their loyalty was as firm as the rock of ages. In all circumstances they upheld us against the carriers. Our word was law. They bowed their heads, and obeyed.

In spite of the dirt, I was secretly rather glad when my cousin decided that we would have to spend a day resting before going on. I had not looked forward to a long march and sat for some time in my hut bathing my feet in Epsom salts dissolved in warm water. After that we sat on our chairs in front of the hut and got out our books. As a child I had often had to play a complicated game which involved answering a great many questions. I was never very interested in the game, for it seemed to me that the questions were too academic, and too useless for everyday life. But one of the questions was, I remember, "If you had to spend the rest of your life on a desert island, what two books would you take, and why?" One of my cousins once slightly enlivened the game with a small flash of wit by answering, "Lamb and Bacon." But in my answers I never rose to anything higher than the heavily obvious. My time had been wasted, I had apparently learnt absolutely nothing from the game. So far as I remember, no one ever suggested Saki or Somerset Maugham. But nevertheless I think the choice was not entirely foolish, for though they interested me they demanded no great concentration from a tired brain. But they certainly had their limitations. One read through them too quickly. It would have been better to have taken some more ambitious book my mind could have struggled with while I was still fresh, and to have been able to keep the short stories for later. But I had no other books with me. Graham was soon deep in the *Anatomy of Melancholy*. I had already read right through the stories of Saki and Somerset Maugham, and now bored and listlessly I started again at the beginning.

The villagers crowded round us. They pinched my arms to see what my white skin felt like. Their great staring eyes watched every movement. They gaped at me as I wrote in my diary, as I bent to tie up my shoe lace, or when the dust in my throat made me choke. And they rose as one man when the demands of nature made me wish to disappear into the bush alone for a moment. It was a long path that led down into the forest, but they followed, silent and curious. I turned round and said irritably: "Shoo! Go away!" and waved my arms. They stared, and the children crept closer. I called my cousin to bring his camera. He stood and guarded my way while I dashed into the bush. The children watched him lifting up the little black box, and then, screaming, they ran away.

My eyes left my book. I had read several pages without taking in a single word of what I was reading. I had not, after all, come all this way to read short stories several times over. There was surely something in this wretched village that could amuse or distract me; something that was not entirely repellent.

Our cook was preparing some fish that he had managed to get hold of somehow for our lunch. He sat in the road absorbed in his work, like a priest preparing a sacrifice. The expression on his face was intent and uplifted. He was not disturbed by the scraggy, unhealthy dogs which came up and sniffed at the fish, but nonchalantly put out his hand and pushed them away. Neither did he mind the skinny chickens scratching in the dust, or the goats that bumped up against him and got in his way. All round him the dust was blowing in little clouds through the village. We could not help fearing that this peculiarly unpleasant sight might spoil our appetites for the food he was preparing with such care, so we asked him to move somewhere where we could not see him. Seriously he collected his things together and shuffled off in his long white robes, a little stream of goats and dogs following him.

Our carriers enjoyed the village, for they had nothing to do all day and the chief had given them good food. I envied them their ability of being entirely idle without boredom. They could sit, leaning against the sides of the huts for hours, doing nothing, saying nothing and, I am convinced, thinking nothing. They were contented, for they lived in the moment, and just then they had everything they wanted—the burning sun on their skins, enough to eat and plenty of companionship. And they also had the monkey to keep them amused. It sat all day on Mark's head, and hissed and spat when Laminah came near it with his irritating tricks. Its little bloodshot eyes glimmered with hate, and Mark would take it off his head for a few moments and pet it and give it a banana to eat.

It seemed a long day, for nothing happened. From time to time we moved our chairs a little bit, for the sun was blinding and we tried to keep in the shade. As we moved, all our audience moved too. Graham gave a very old man a cigarette. He spluttered and choked, and the tears rolled down his cheeks as he tried to smoke it, and then he passed it on. A wave of life passed over the group round us as long as the cigarette lasted, and then died down like a puff of wind on a summer's day. It was very hot, and I had not yet got used to the smell of black bodies.

The chief came and sat near us, and his eyes glistened greedily as he saw the whisky bottle. My cousin, remembering the food he had given the carriers, gave him a drink as a sign of gratitude. The chief tossed it off, and in less than a second he was blind drunk. He got up unsteadily, and muttering and dribbling he tottered round the village. We saw him rolling off to his hut, and we were not sorry to see the last of him. He was a nasty, depraved old man, with a crafty, mean face, and obviously at some time must have known civilisation of the coast. There was nothing simple and unspoilt about this village. It was twisted and bad. There was an atmosphere of decay everywhere. One could feel it, see it, and smell it. Even the children were like horrid old men, and their wicked little faces grinned at us. I felt that if we stayed in this village much longer we, too, would deteriorate and go bad, the atmosphere of degeneration was so strong. It was all round us and touched us closely. It lay in the air we breathed and in the food we ate. How this loathsome unhealthiness had crept in I do not know, but I could only suppose that it had come up somehow from the semi-civilisation of the coast. I kept looking at Graham to see if I could see any change beginning in him, for I could not understand how we could escape being contaminated. I thought I might see that shameful, shameless look creep into his eyes. I half expected his face to alter, and his body to become diseased and horrible like those around us. The unlovely nakedness pressing so close to me filled me with repulsion. It disgusted me. There was nc beauty, no freshness, in the village anywhere.

Night came at last. We ate our supper in front of the gaping crowds, and drank whisky. We would like to have entered a state of sweet forgetfulness, to feel the sharp edges blurred. It would be pleasant if, for the rest of the evening, we could lose this sense of quivering disgust at the sore bodies around us—if we could rise above them or, at any rate, feel sympathy for them. But the whisky seemed to have no effect on us at all. We drank again, and thought of our friends in London, and wondered what they were doing, and where they were. I began to get that feeling of being outside my own body, and I watched from afar those two little white creatures in the heart of Liberia among the dirt and filth. Two small white puppets, pulled by strings out of their usual course, and dragged hither and thither into incongruous situations. Two white dolls sitting stiffly on absurd green canvas chairs, drinking whisky, and wondering where the strings would pull them to next. So useless, so ineffective—just paper dolls who would soon pass on and leave the rotting village to decay and die.

The hours crawled by, and at last it was late enough to go to bed. It was another sleepless, fearful night among the rats. I lay awake, but desperately tired, and longed for the grey light of the dawn to come creeping into my hut.

We left Duogobmai next morning as early as possible, and walked away from it with no regrets in our hearts. It was a beautiful morning, although it soon got very hot, and the walk was pleasant. Graham raced on ahead as usual, but I sauntered. The men were in a good mood and sang their strange songs without stopping. We walked through thick forest, but the track was easy, and the way was much shorter than I had imagined it would be. We could have walked only eight or nine miles when we arrived at Nicoboozu, and I felt quite fresh as I walked into the village.

Nicoboozu was a charming place and beautifully clean. The huts were far apart from one another, and the spaces in between were swept. All through the village we could hear the sounds of laughter and gaiety. We were in the heart of the Buzie country, which is supposed to be the only artistic tribe of Liberia, although until we came to this village we had seen no signs of their culture. Here everything was beautiful. The bases of the huts were painted with strange designs. The village blacksmith made rings and bracelets out of old Napoleon coins which were still to be found in French Guinea, and which were brought over into Liberia by the wandering tribe, the Mandingos. The women also wore beautiful little ornaments in their fuzzy black hair. There were men busy weaving cloth on their primitive looms. The patterns were simple, effective, and unselfconscious. They wove the material in long strips, securing one end with a heavy stone, which they moved farther and farther from the loom as they went on weaving. The people, artistic by nature, were incapable of making ugly things. The spearheads and swords were most delicately carved.

It was impossible not to feel happy. Our one grumbling porter had left us, and we had got one in his place who loved to sing. It was agony to him to keep silent. He was a member of the Buzie tribe, and all the time his voice could be heard lifted up in weird, monotonous songs.

The village was a wonderful contrast from Duogobmai. We were welcomed enthusiastically by the men and women. They flocked round us, merry and high-spirited, chattering as madly as birds at dawn. The women felt the material of my shorts, rubbing it between their fingers like women at a bargain sale. The men stood round smiling. With very few exceptions did the men of the country ever look upon me with special interest as a woman. To them I was just some white creature, strange and curious perhaps, but not in the least sexually exciting. I could have wandered round by myself with perfect safety.

In a way, I suppose, my cousin and I were a kind of circus to the natives, an unexpected amusement brought suddenly into their lives for a day or two. On those occasions when I had a hut to myself at night I had no fear at all that my slumbers might be disturbed by the Don Juan of the village. The first time, I confess, I had wondered whether I should have the revolver within reach, but as I occasionally walk or do odd things in my sleep, I thought on the whole it might be better kept under lock and key in the money-box. But I quickly realised that my appeal was non-existent, and though in any other circumstances my pride might have been hurt, in Liberia I could but feel profoundly thankful!

The village girls crowded into my hut with me and watched with great interest while I changed my shirt and washed. I did not mind their being there. They were charming, and smiled at me so excitedly and shyly. When I washed myself they could not understand what the soap was, but loved the way it made the water fluffy. They dipped the tips of their fingers into it when I had finished, and then gazed at the bubbles as they gradually disappeared. I broke off a small corner of the soap and gave them a piece, and it was passed round eagerly from hand to hand, till one of them tried to eat it. They stroked my arms, not rudely and inquisitively as they had done it at the last village, but gently, which I learnt later was a sign of approval. Although we could exchange no word, we laughed together and felt friendly and happy.

The women had their breasts, and sometimes the whole of their bodies down to the waist, cut in strange patterns during their time in bush school. Some of the very young girls in this village were quite lovely; they held their heads high and moved gracefully. But disease soon ravaged their bodies. The older women looked gaunt and withered, and unattractive in their nakedness. But in spite of the sores and the unhealthiness there was a freshness in the village, a cleanliness of spirit, and a charm that came straight from the heart. Their manners were good and dignified. The women realised at once when I no longer wanted to have them near me, and gracefully they withdrew and left me alone. Somehow we came very near to understanding one another, and I felt I was among people I liked.

I went out and wandered round the village. It was similar to all other villages. It was set on a clearing on the top of the hill, and down below I could see the river. In the centre of the village there was the usual palaver-house, a hut with open sides, where any kind of meetings and discussions could be held. The blacksmith was working in his smithy. I did not at that time know how important a man the blacksmith was—more important than the chief himself—but I noticed that the men and women gathered round his fire for a chat and a gossip.

A curious smell spread through the whole village. It was unlike anything I had ever smelt in Europe. It was heavy and nauseating. I had noticed it already sometimes on our trip, but it was only at Nicoboozu that I learnt that it was the food for our men that smelt in this un-appetising way.

The chief roused himself from his slumbers and asked us to come and inspect it. There were eight enormous bowls of rice covered with an evil-smelling, bright yellow sauce, with odd lumps of meat or fish thrown on the top. It was a most revolting sight, but our men's eyes brightened. It was their one meal of the day. In our ignorance at first we occasionally allowed them to eat in the mornings, before we started on the day's march. We soon learnt that those invariably were bad days. The men were not used to two meals a day, and it made them lazy and ill-tempered. That night they were delighted with what they received. "Plenty fine chop," said Mark greedily, as he elbowed himself into a place by one of the bowls. The men crouched over their food, hollowed out their right hands into a kind of spoon, mixed up the food in the bowl, and stuffed their mouths full. There was no talking or laughing while they ate. It was a very serious business. Hurriedly they crammed themselves up with food, chewed it quickly and stuffed it down, and then, satiated, they got up slowly; cheerful and good-natured.

Graham and I had our supper. It was one of our happiest evenings together—one of the last times when we could talk completely naturally to one another, without wondering whether anything we said could possibly hurt the other in any way. So soon after that we had to give up discussing subjects on which we held different points of view. It sounds unbelievably childish now, but in our weariness we got easily impatient with arguments. My tiredness made my brain work even more slowly than it usually does, and I would grope unsuccessfully for the words I needed. Sometimes as I was in the very middle of saying something my strength would give out and I would murmur weakly, "I expect you're right, really," which must have irritated my cousin profoundly. Graham, on the other hand, would sometimes become rather obstinate, hanging on to some small, unimportant point like a dog to a bone. But we never quarrelled, not once. We knew so well that it was the ghastly damp heat that was lowering our vitality, and we would smile at one another and think, "We won't talk about that again." Politics was the first thing to go. I sometimes heard myself expressing the most extraordinary ideas, professing the strangest beliefs. Words would come out of my mouth which had nothing to do with my own thoughts. I would listen to the tired voice, and think, "What an odd thing to say." Sometimes what I was saying would sound so dull that I could hardly bear to hear it myself, and I would lose interest in the middle of a sentence. So many unfinished sentences; so many words; sounds trailing away into nothingness and floating off into the hot, moist air. One subject after another would be put away, left on one side, marked carefully, "Not wanted during voyage," till gradually practically nothing remained on the last day or two of our trip except the enthralling subject of food. By that time, of course, it was the one thing above all others that really interested us, and we found that we did not irritate each other by longing for different kinds of food. But those days were still to come. In Nicoboozu we did not even guess that they would ever come. We were feeling so well, and not yet tired, and our minds were fresh.

Both of us were enchanted with the village, happy and completely under the spell of the African night.

Rather messily with our hands we squeezed out some limes, added a little whisky and pretended that we were drinking ice-cold cocktails. We lingered over our meal. Our cook had made us an enormous omelette, opened a tin of something for our second course, and with a lack of imagination that was unusual for him, he made another large omelette, which, however, he called a pancake. Amadu, Laminah, and Mark served us with the greatest dignity and care, as if we were dining at some important function in London. The food that they placed before us might have been the most rare, the most exotic dishes. My shorts felt shorter than ever. An evening gown and orchids would have fitted better with their manner.

We ate in front of our hut, and as we were eating, the daylight disappeared with tropical suddenness, and night fell. It was a warm night, but not too hot. A small moon appeared in the sky, and the little white huts shone in the silver light around us. An unreal light, rather theatrical. I began quite suddenly to feel the over-whelming magic of Africa. Its strange charm crept over me. Like a drug it gets into the brain and sends it to sleep, so that nothing remains alive but the senses. The warmth flows into one's limbs, the music of the harps into the soul, the timelessness into the spirit, and the rest is perfect well-being and a tremendous peace. I wanted to hang on to the minute. It was one of those moments in life when one is standing on tiptoe, afraid to move or breathe for fear one might break the spell; one of those precious times when one feels, "I am perfectly happy."

I was conscious of it as I was sitting there in the dark. At that moment I wanted nothing more, nothing different in any way.

The women were walking through the village carrying glowing wood from the smithy with which to light the fires they always had in their huts during the night, and gradually through the door of every hut could be seen little leaping flames. All round us were the sounds of tinkling harps. Our carriers were sitting together laughing and contented, drinking palm wine.

There was a breathless moment of hesitation in the air, as if time for once was standing still so that we might absorb the moment; to give us this one chance to fill ourselves to the utmost with peace and beauty.

A few women came and danced in front of us. They were led by a hideous old hag, who cackled as she twisted and shook her withered body to the rhythm of the rattles. It was, to our ideas, an ugly dance, and even the youngest of the women could not succeed in looking graceful as she stuck out her behind and kicked out her legs. But they were merry and gay. They danced in a small circle, with their fingers held out straight, and slapped their thighs in time to the music. Their movements were awkward and jerky, but they laughed and, as they danced, they called out jokes to each other.

After that there was more dancing. The moon goes to the heads of the natives like strong wine. All night they danced. The men began and the women moved to one side and watched. One could feel the excitement. Sometimes they let out strange little shouts. They stamped their feet and clapped their bodies with their

hands. Even the children feel the strong influence of
the moon, and the little naked piccaninnies were hopping
madly round between the houses. Later, as the moon
waned, we saw less and less dancing, but that night they
were drunk with it.

I would like to linger over this evening, but there is
nothing more one can say. Nothing happened. There
was no sense of anticlimax. It was something perfect in
itself. There was a moon and a native village, dancing,
and naked black babies laughing. There were two white
people watching and having their arms stroked from time
to time. There was friendliness, and gaiety that came
straight from the heart. And, wonder of wonders, there
was a hut that night with no rats!

# CHAPTER V

THE road to Zigiter next day wound steadily up into the hills. Almost on hands and knees we scrambled over rocks and boulders, climbing up and up. Our feet would slip on the narrow, rough little track, and plants and roots would trip us up or cling to our clothes and drag us back. On each side of us was thick, untidy bush, and the high trees nearly joined in a kind of archway over our heads. The atmosphere was damp and hot, and no light breeze could reach us. I was gasping slightly, for it was hard to breathe, and I felt as if someone were hammering iron nails into my throat. I did not know how far it was to Zigiter, and I was afraid to drink very much from my water-bottle. I never stopped to look into the bush each side of me, my eyes were on the ground in front and my mind was fully concentrated on what I was doing. My hands felt sore with pulling myself over the steepest bits.

I felt like some poor creature in a Walt Disney film, wending a heartbreakingly cruel way up a twisty, winding road to the wicked castle lying high up on the mountain-side. The bad plants clung to me evilly with their thin, long, black fingers, and occasionally a snake would glide sinuously across the path. The mischievous rocks would loosen as they felt my weight upon them. They would break away and go crashing down the hill, almost dragging me with them, and I felt that if I listened carefully I would be able to hear their mocking laughter. Sometimes a monkey, high up above me, would throw down something that would just miss me, and when I looked up to swear at it, it would swing carelessly out of my sight. And in the meantime the good little plants sighed softly, and the pretty little butterflies fluttered helplessly round. What chance had innocence against these overpowering forces of evil? Such futile weakness against so much strength?

Up and up we climbed, up the Disney road into the centre, into the very heart of the evil spirits. And suddenly we saw Zigiter above us, not as a magic castle, but yet unreal with all the unearthly charm of the native villages. It lay on the very top of a big rock, one of the highest points in Liberia. We climbed up, and all round us on the horizon lay a circle of hills, separated by deep, thickly wooded valleys and oddly shaped grey crags such as El Greco loved to paint. We could see for miles. It was one of the few times that we ever had a good view. I stretched my eyes over the valleys and shook off the feeling of suffocation that gently strangles one in a forest. A forest at any time is too big and overpowering to be happy in. It shows one too clearly what one is in the world—a little scrap of nothing at all. Surrounded by our men, I lifted up my eyes unto the hills, and began to feel once again that I was a human being, with a place, however obscure, in the scheme of things. The hills looked peaceful enough, but soon we were to see them lit up in a storm, to see the fierce, garish, tropical lightning fly from hill to crag, from crag to hill. A magnificent, exciting scene of the uncontrolled passions of the gods.

Zigiter was the biggest town of the Buzie tribe; the centre, not of Buzie culture, but of Buzie sorcery, witchcraft and magic. Where strange arts were practised, and the wickedest, blackest medicines were understood. Where the women learnt, in their bush schools, the dark secrets of poisoning. Where it was said that the art of throwing lightning was well known. And where all the people lived under the shadow of ghastly unknown influences.

There was a Liberian District Commissioner stationed at Zigiter. He was away, but by the time I arrived Graham had already seen the town chief and arranged with him to let us have a house on the compound. It was a big house with two rooms, divided by a kind of central hall. Our carriers were given a hut at the back, where they slept and where the cook prepared our meals. But when we first arrived they threw themselves on the ground around us and rested in our house.

Graham, contrary to all the advice that he had received in Freetown from the Europeans, had an excellent method of his own for dealing with the men. We had been told that it was useless to expect obedience or honesty unless we showed by the most primitive methods what strong masters we were. Blacks, we had been told, would only respect a yelling voice and a heavy hand, and that if we once lost their respect we would be done for. They would steal our things, they would mutiny, they would try to do us down over money. They would desert us in the bush without a qualm if they felt like it. In fact there was nothing they would not do if once they lost their fear of us. Graham, however, from the beginning treated them exactly as if they were white men from our own country. He talked to them quite naturally and they liked him. They knew where they were with him, and apart from their everlasting cries of "Too far," they did everything he wanted them to do. His method of conversation was far from simple, and he used long, complicated phrases. I do not believe that the men ever understood him, but after a while they began to get some dim idea of what he was driving at. After the day's trek they would like to lie round him, and joke and laugh, while he, like a benevolent father, would smile kindly upon them. Once away from their own country the men depended so much on us. They knew they were going to Monrovia, but what or where Monrovia was they had no idea. But with child-like simplicity they handed all responsibilities over to my cousin, quite sure that he would look after them and see that they came to no harm. Their naïvety was their most endearing quality. They were so sure that we would be pleased to see them at any time. They would come to us with a pain or a cut during our meals, and they would interrupt our conversations to ask us to settle one of their foolish quarrels. Our ugliest, most hideous porter brought me a little bouquet of flowers every morning to pin on the front of my shirt, for he had observed me doing it one morning. With a shy grin that crumpled up his entire face he would present it to me, and I would express my thanks with smiles and bows. They were charming to us, and we got to know them all so well.

After we had rested, our carriers spread the word that we were ready to buy jewellery, swords and daggers while we were still in the Buzie country, and every man in the village came up to us with things they were ready to sell. Graham and I sat in our chairs while the natives spread their wares at our feet. My boy, Laminah, stood at my elbow and helped me to bargain. At first the natives brought us rubbish, for they saw we were ignorant and foolish creatures, but our boys guarded us with determination, refusing to let us lose face before our carriers. "No buy, Missis," Laminah would whisper. "Dat man plenty big humbug. No good sword." And I would wave it away scornfully, as if surprised that they should bring me such trash.

Gradually it dawned on the natives that we were not going to buy rubbish, and away they all went, returning presently with their real treasures—swords that had been in the family for generations, daggers that were heirlooms. They were valuable weapons to them, too, for with their spears and bows and arrows they were the only weapons they were allowed to possess. But the lure of money was great, and when temptation was dangled before their eyes they fell. The bargaining began, and the blood of Laminah was roused. These uncivilised natives were not going to get the better of him. He laughed to scorn the prices they asked, offered a minute sum, and when they finally agreed to accept it, cut down his offer by half again. One ferocious-looking man got angry and said that Laminah knew too much, but Laminah beat down this man too and got his sword for us at his own price. Next day, however, he came to us full of fears. The angry man with whom he had argued was the devil's head man, and it was not good in this village to go against the devil. The natives finally went away, and left the pile of things spread out on the floor. We looked them through, and spent a pleasant and exciting half-hour dividing them between us by tossing for them. Our boys were very glad that we had bought some swords, for presently we would be going through a wilder country and they would be our only protection should anything happen. By this time I felt fairly sure that nothing unexpected would turn up that would necessitate our drawing our swords, but it was pleasant to feel that we could make our boys happy so easily. I had once for a very short time learnt fencing, but I did not feel confident that, should the occasion arise, I should be able to make use of my small knowledge of this art. And try as I would, I could not imagine my cousin in a Douglas Fairbanks role, fencing skilfully against a score of angry natives. Though Amadu would stand by our sides ready to die with us, Laminah, I felt sure, would run away in any crisis, and would only return when all danger to life and limb was over. He would then of course be quite ready to boast of all the imaginary difficulties he had overcome, but that would be very little help. The cook would certainly go on with his cooking. So I felt the swords would never be marked with blood. I would never, when I came back to England, be able to point to dark and grue-some stains, and make the curly hair of my small nephews rise on end with horror while I told sad stories of the death of chiefs. But our boys were happy, and strapped the swords round their shoulders, and Mark and Laminah found infinite enjoyment in cutting off small boughs as we walked through the forest.

Our men came to us with their usual aches and pains, which we had to tend every evening. Like children they came to us, pointing out their hurts with the utmost confidence that we could make them well again. Most of our medical supplies had been left at Freetown in the last-minute rush, but we had plenty of Epsom salts that we used for most things, some boric acid tablets, and some iodine. We had a good deal of quinine with us, but that we kept for ourselves, for we had to take a strong dose of it every day. Our men would come to us with sore throats; one of them had nasty venereal sores, another had yaws. One of them came to me with a badly cut toe one day. Our bandages had got lost, but I tore up a handkerchief and tied up his toe with a big bow on top. He was as pleased as Punch, and showed it with the utmost pride to every one; and kept it on, black with dirt, long after the toe had healed. The villagers would come to us, too, in great numbers, with touching faith in the white man's medicine, and we would give them a few grains of Epsom salts and a lot of hocus-pocus talk of what they were to do with them.

That evening in Zigiter a man came and stood in front of Graham, silently holding out his hands. I saw his face first, noticed his eyes dumbly pleading for hope, frightened and bewildered. I watched him staring at my cousin, urging him, willing him to give him some sort of help. I looked at his hands. They were the rotting hands of a leper, already in a very bad state. My cousin gravely, and without showing by the flicker of an eyelash what he must surely have felt, gave the man some medicine. The man took it with shining eyes. He turned and went away with a firm step. It meant at least one day of happiness for him.

We went into the hut and sat together in the central room in the half light, talking quietly to each other, waiting for our supper. There was a slight rustle, the mat hanging in front of the door was pushed aside, and a man entered. He slid in like a snake, and stood silently in a corner. My cousin asked him sharply what he wanted. He answered in almost incomprehensible English that we were not to leave the house that night. The Big Bush Devil whom no one may see was going to dance through the village that night. We were not to go out. We were not to look out. We would hear the big drum beating and we would then stay in our house. He looked at me, turned his eyes slowly to Graham and then slipped out of the door again, in the same snake-like way he had come in.

It was hot and breathless. The storm that was to break out with such force the next day made the air heavy and oppressive. It was a damp heat, and though we were sitting still, every few moments we had to wipe away the perspiration from our faces. It was an evening full of atmosphere, when nothing seems too strange to be believed.

I had a sudden stab of pain in my foot. I had caught another jigger and my foot was burning sharply, so I called my boy to come and cut the noisome insect out for me.

Laminah was very subdued as he knelt before me,

hacking and squeezing the little jigger out of my toe. Zigiter terrified him. He had heard already that the devil no one may see was going to dance through the village, and he was afraid that we would be foolish and not obey orders.

"Do you really think anything can happen to us?" we asked. "Devil plenty afraid of white man."

"Massa go blind. Missis go blind. All go blind," and shaking with fear he went on operating on my foot, holding the sharp little knife in his trembling hand.

We called Amadu. It was strange that Laminah who had lived all his life in Freetown and had always worked for white men, could so quickly become as superstitious and as primitive in his outlook as our simplest carrier. He made no attempt to hide his fear. He was not ashamed of it. There were bad things that could happen in this village and he knew it.

Amadu was even more serious than usual. He explained to us quietly how easy it would be to put poison in the carriers' food, should we be observed peeping out of the house. It was necessary for the devil to punish us if we did not obey him, otherwise how could he keep up his power? Suddenly, without warning, his self-control went, and excitedly the words came pouring out of his mouth in a long and complicated story of what the devil could do if he was angry. A story he knew was true. It happened in 1923. The devil had made himself invisible, and had walked straight through a table, cutting it in half and leaving the people on each side blind.

They brought us our supper. We could feel them

silently urging us to eat more quickly, not to have a second helping, praying that we would refuse the sweet. They pulled the mosquito blinds down in front of the windows and drew the mat carefully in front of the door so that there were no chinks we could see through. As soon as we had finished eating they disappeared into their little hut with the other men. We looked out at the back. They had hung something in front of the window and were sitting in complete silence. Not a movement, not a sound could we hear, but their nervousness and fear hung eerily in the still air.

Devil or no devil, it was necessary for us to go out and disappear into the bush once more before retiring for the night. If the big drum should start to beat before we got back, well, by all accounts it would be too bad for someone. But the laws of nature are strong and must be obeyed, and out we went.

We took an electric torch with us and sallied forth. There was not a light to be seen in the village. No little flickering lights shining inside the huts, for each hut had something hung across the doorway. It was like a village of the dead. It was quiet and we could hear no voices chattering or laughing. The heavy, windless night pressed down on our heads. As we walked we became conscious of soft footsteps following us. We turned and flashed our torch about us, but could see nothing. There is something nerve-racking in being followed by something one cannot see. I had even one night in a civilised German town worked myself into a state of terror when I thought I heard footsteps behind me that walked as I walked, stopped when I stopped, and finally ran as I ran.

That might easily have been an echo, but here it was real. There was someone slinking behind us, hidden in the shadows. We were so helpless. We came back through the silent village. We could see nothing. The footsteps followed us up to the house.

It was difficult not to feel jumpy. There was something going on that we could not understand, and that we were unable to investigate. We could not face this thing squarely face to face. It was something that lived in the shadows, and ruled through mystery and terror. Through the evil it could do to our men it became our master too, and we must needs bow to its laws, and obey. Nervousness is the most catching thing in the world. Against all one's reasoning, and against one's will, it creeps up and catches one by the throat. We could hear the footsteps creeping round the house now, softly and slowly.

Suddenly the devil's music began. Drums beating, first softly and then louder and louder. Rhythmically. Insistent.

Graham and I sat in our little house. It seemed undignified to have to obey such primitive commands, and in spite of everything we were intensely curious to see what was going on. We put out the light, crept softly to the window, lifted a little corner of the blind and peeped out. My heart was beating. There was so much they could do to us, but I was very intrigued to see what was going on. We looked down towards the devil's house. We could see nothing. The whole village was dark. We let down the blind again. In a few moments we heard the footsteps pass the window again.

I went to bed, but before I did so I walked right round the room to see if anyone could be lurking in some dark corner. The devil would certainly have sent someone to watch us, for in all this village we were the only ones likely to try to find out what was going on. I found nothing in my room, but it was easy enough to slip in and out of the house past the mat over the door, and I went to sleep feeling that there was someone, somewhere, who could see me. Next day our men were upset when we told them that we were going to have a day of rest at Zigiter. They were very subdued, and for once they were ready to press on, while we wished to stay.

The sharp contrasts in the atmospheres of the various villages we had passed through in Liberia were very strange. In Duogobmai the atmosphere had been sordid and degenerate. In Nicoboozu it was happy and charming, and here in Zigiter, even in the light of morning, it was evil. We could not tell at that time which was the most characteristic village, but as we went on we found that until we came near the coast that it was the villages with the spirit of Nicoboozu that predominated. Duogobmai had slipped into the interior of Liberia out of its right place. And Zigiter was unique, the gathering point of all Buzie superstitions. The devil here was a bad devil, and had the entire village under his thumb. Instead of being a help and a teacher, a kind of good-natured schoolmaster, he was a tyrant, and the natives lived in the shadow of fear. The devil's headman and the devil's medicine man had strong powers that they used for their own ends. One could readily understand that any native who disobeyed their commands could so easily be dragged out into the bush and never be heard of again. The artistic natures of the Buzie tribe make them at the same time the most superstitious. Zigiter had a District Commissioner from Monrovia. We did not see him, but it was apparent that his influence was weak, and that it was the devil who ruled the town.

They were building a new house for the devil. It was big and magnificent, and the entire village was busy carrying up buckets of water from the river to make the clay walls. I went down with my camera to take some pictures, and soon Mark came tearing after me.

"Come away, Missis. Come away," he said, with terror in his eyes. "This very bad place. They no fight with swords. They no fight with knife. They fight with very bad medicine. They depend on bad medicine."

He insisted on my coming up to the house with him, and when we got there he gave his shy little laugh and disappeared.

Amadu begged us not to laugh at the devil, for he could make himself invisible and hear all we said. We asked him why he was so scared, he was a Mohammedan and had a God. "Massa has a God, but no devil," he explained. "I have God, but plenty devils too."

All through the morning we could hear the thunder rumbling round the country-side. By the devil's house a man was standing waving a long brush of elephant hair to keep the coming storm away from the house. Suddenly the storm burst. The heavens opened and like a solid lump the rain came down on us. It was not yet the season for the rains, but this year they seemed to be starting early. The man outside the devil's house did not move. With admirable optimism he stood there in the downpour, waving away the storm, for hours on end. We stood on the verandah and watched the lightning. The thunder roared like an angry lion round the hills. All day it went on, and into the night. In the darkness the crags were lit up in flaming fantastic lights.

The devil's headman came to us and demanded kerosene. It was sheer blackmail, for he showed us by his manner that he knew we would not dare refuse. Laminah, still full of fears, wanted to give him all we had. Like a frightened school-boy he wanted to pacify the big bully with presents and soft speeches. Graham interrupted, gave the man a little, and told him that was all we could spare. Laminah watched, his expression a strange mixture of respect and fear, at this exhibition of bravery.

Again we were told the devil wished to dance through the village, and we were not to go out. But the storm had burst, and the nervous tension had snapped. The excitement and feeling of suspense had gone. Normal reactions reasserted themselves and odd feelings and fancies fled away. We were no longer nervous, but a little grain of superstition remained in our minds. For a time we had been carried away and had almost believed in strange supernatural things. We had got so near believing that even now we were saying, "How do we know that it is impossible to throw lightning at people just because we can't do it in England?" "Why shouldn't the devil be able to make himself invisible, or, at any rate, by some means of thought-reading be able to find out what we are saying and thinking?" "Who is the devil, anyway? Is he a real man? If he is, is it only the headman and the medicine man who know who he is? Or is it only an idea, a power that does not really exist, but is forced on the natives by the heads of the village, by terrifying methods?" There were so many things we could not understand, and that our boys would not tell us. So many riddles without an answer. So many things we wanted to know, and that were only told us much later by tired, nervous, world-weary Dr. Harley in Ganta.

Our fear left us and that night we peeped out for quite a long time from the window. But everything was dark. The storm still raged, and by the flares of lightning we could see the devil's new house in the distance. We watched it carefully. The drums began their strange, monotonous noise; there were rattles, and we could hear shouting. But nothing came out of the house. We could see no one. The rain poured down. The little white huts were closed up. There was no dancing and no singing. Our men remained silently in their hut. It was a tiny hut, and how thirty men could crush into it I could not imagine. They must have been lying on top of one another, too terrified to move or complain, hot and uncomfortable. I went to bed. Before I fell asleep I could hear footsteps creeping round the house. I was no longer nervous, but for the rest of the trip a thought nagged incessantly at me in my brain. Should we have looked out of the window? Had anyone seen us? For from that day Graham never felt really well again. Whether it was the power of ideas over the body or whether it was already the beginning of his illness I do not know. But from that last evening at Zigiter his health began to suffer, and for the rest of the trip and even for sometime after he got to England again, he was unwell.

I fell into a heavy sleep, but as I woke from time to time during the night the rats, playing so noisily round my bed, got muddled up with my fantastic dreams of bogies and witches.

# CHAPTER VI

SHE was waiting for us when we arrived at Zorzor, for we had sent on a messenger to say we were coming. A large white lump, like bread before it is put in the oven to be baked. One felt that should one press her she would sink in and the dent would remain for ever. Someone had put two black currants into the dough for eyes, and her mouth was an old strip of orange peel. Solid and heavy, and when baked, bad for the digestion. Her grey hair stood out in wisps like an old wig brought out of the acting box to amuse the children on a rainy afternoon. Her shapeless, faded cotton dress was fastened modestly, but untidily, at the throat with a large safety pin. Her podgy little hands fluttered about her in nervous, weary gestures while she spoke, pulling down the back of her skirt, clutching the neck of her dress, or merely waving aimlessly in the air.

She was the missionary at Zorzor. She lived alone, miles and miles from any other white human being. Her husband had been drowned one day in Monrovia, and the other man who had been with them had long ago gone off his head and been removed. She stayed on. There was nothing else she could do. She had been there so long. She could not retire and go back to America, for what could she do there? She had no friends there now, and no money. This had been her work, her life. She must stay on.

She stood there, this large white lump of lifeless humanity, and welcomed us in her own fashion. Her voice seemed to come from a long way off, floated uncertainly towards us, and then floated off again on a high, whining note:

"I'd have sent you an invite to dinner, but I'm going home in six months time. . . ." The words faded out, and her arms flapped round her vaguely.

We walked over to a big dusty, wooden shed, which she said was to be our rest-house. She sighed as she walked: deep, unconscious sighs. But she could not concentrate. She found that she had forgotten the keys, and she looked round her absently, her hands moving this way and that, as if she expected the keys to drop into them from heaven.

"Are you really alone here?" asked my cousin. She gazed at him. He looked dirty, unshaven, and tough. Her face went blanker even than it had been before, and she turned away without answering, apparently afraid in a dim kind of way, of ideas that she vaguely thought might lie in his mind.

We trailed round the house. We were all whining now. Perhaps my cousin and I had been whining for days, but we had not been conscious of it till we heard her voice. It was the heat. Energy withered up and died, like a delicate plant in a drought.

Her hands moved vaguely round the untidy, musty room, indicating an old table, a broken chair, a window with a torn mosquito wire. She looked at us as if she hardly expected to see us still there, and whined, "I guess we try to keep it free of bugs." And she drifted off, white, solid, and unsmiling to her own house.

But I had seen something that gladdened my heart. I suddenly became fiercely greedy, and I was determined not to say a word about my discovery till I had seen whether there was enough for two. If there was not much there, I would keep it all for myself. I would use it all and not give one drop away.

I could hardly wait to be alone, but for the moment it was impossible. One of our carriers was sick. I felt guilty and blamed myself for having looked out of the window the night before. He was very bad and asked to go home. He was a good, quiet boy, and seemed sorry to leave us. We paid him his money sadly, and we did not dare to give him a tip, for it was the promise of a present to anyone who stayed with us to the end, that was keeping the carriers faithful. Graham, too, felt unwell.

At last I was alone, and I went straight to the corner where I had seen it. I was as happy as if I had found hidden treasure. It was a large bottle of lysol, and it was half full. I poured it recklessly into my washing water and washed myself till I smelt like a hospital, but felt cleaner than I had done for many a long day. I was more pleased than if I had found the most exotic bath-salts. I gave what I did not use to Graham, feeling generous. I was feeling most extraordinarily well. My feet had nearly healed and were getting beautifully hard. The long walks seemed to suit me, and although the heat was almost too much of a good thing, it now seemed to tire my mind only and not my body. I was getting used to being bitten all over by insects and just went on scratching automatically, thankful that although they bit every other part of my body, they never attacked my face.

Our house was full of tracts, pamphlets, and sentimental stories for children. Stories that must have been completely incomprehensible to the natives in the wilds, for they dealt entirely with things of everyday life in America. But most of them looked as if they had never been used. They lay in great dusty heaps on the floor and were probably brought out many years before, when the missionaries first came out. They were now nothing but the pathetic reminders of the things that the good missionaries had hoped, in their dense, well-meaning way, to accomplish. They were tales of such sugary sweetness that they made me feel sick. I put them away from me. They were not even funny.

Every now and then I saw the missionary. She kept a black baby in her house and was looking after it vaguely and inefficiently, but with great kindness. Gradually I felt that underneath all that suffocating, woolly exterior there lay a big heart. But the heat and loneliness were getting her down. She kept a cobra in her garden, which she fed on a chicken a day. She thought it would be fun to see the cobra swallow the chicken one day, but so far she had never been able to organise it so that she came out to watch at the right time. Otherwise I do not know what she did all day. I suppose she held services somewhere, or perhaps she had a little school. Or perhaps she just trailed round in her expressionless, absent way, flapping her arms.

Graham went over to her house during the evening to consult with her about routes. He took some of the carriers with him so that they might get instructions they could understand. They sat in her stuffy sitting-room round a big fire. She knew nothing, of course, had forgotten long ago anything she had ever known, and could remember the names of no villages. But she called a guide, and Graham then decided to go to Bama-kama in French Guinea. The guide said he always took two days, but he thought there was a quicker way by Jbaiay, if the road was passable. The missionary's guide and our men talked together, and our carriers became restless. They thought they were going to be made to walk too far again. My cousin said that they would go first to Jbaiay, and then if it was too far to go on we could spend the night there. They murmured among them-selves, and then quite suddenly, with suspicious good humour, agreed.

We got up as soon as it was light next morning, and wanted to be off as soon as possible. But for hours we hung about, waiting for the carriers to pack up our things. They were lazy and tiresome, and demanded another day of rest. They quarrelled among themselves and refused to hurry, so that it was nearly nine o'clock before we left the tumble-down little settlement and the lonely—the desperately lonely—woman.

As I walked a slight horror that I had had at the back of my mind for the last day or two began definitely to take shape. So far I had been able to push it out of sight, but the time had come when it would no longer lie hidden. The truth was that boredom was beginning to rear its

85

ugly head. The sheer, utter boredom of walking for hours on end, when the bush closed in so heavily on either side, that it was impossible to see anything at all. By now I was used to the great towering trees, to the monkeys, to the strings of ants, to the butterflies. It was all the same. There was nothing new. There was nothing more to see. Never a view, never a change. Most of the time it was necessary to keep one's eyes fixed on the path in front, for it was always rough. But if one did raise one's head, what was there to see? Trees, trees, and again trees.

"I'll see if I can think of enough Shakespeare to recite for half an hour," I thought. I looked at the time. Eleven o'clock. Good. "To be or not to be. . . ." On and on. One thing after another till I could think of no more. It must be half an hour. I looked at my watch. Eleven o'clock! I held it up to my ear, furious. My watch, of course, had gone wrong again, as it did nearly every day. I should have been used to it, but I was unbelievably angry. All right. I won't play any more, then. I stamped on. Damn, I shall have to think of something else to think about.

After several hours we stopped for lunch. Graham's watch has also stopped. We have no idea what time it is, but feel that it is getting late. Graham also is furious. He is convinced that the carriers are leading us out of our way, so that we shall not be able to reach Bamakama to-night. I am angry. Graham is angry. And for some reason the carriers are all furious too. We walk on. At last we came to a good-looking, pleasant village. What it was called we never discovered; but Graham was right when he thought that our men were deliberately leading us astray, so that we would not attempt the long walk to Bamakama. We decided to stop for the night, for we had no idea where we were, and to walk on to Bamakama next day, however far it was.

One thing we felt sure of. We were in French Guinea. Even in this backwater there was a different feeling, a more sophisticated atmosphere, than we had been used to. Tall, good-looking Mandingo traders wandered about. They are a wandering tribe, buying goods and junk in one place to sell in another. They travel from the most inland districts down to the coast and back again. All kinds of cheap crockery and other stuff lay round the village in evidence of their industry. The girls walked round with their hair plaited and stiffened into strange coils round their heads. Their bodies, too, were painted, in strips and designs, in strange colours. Every one crowded round us, full of the commercial spirit, wanting to sell us things. One old man tried to sell us a goat, but as we were still trailing about with us the one we had had the whole trip, we refused. Actually our poor goat was living his last few hours on earth, but we did not know that then.

Our carriers were restless and still bad-tempered. They had eaten food in the morning before we started, and that was always a bad thing. They were gathering in little groups muttering. Our boys kept close to us, showing their loyalty in many little ways, so that I knew we had serious trouble ahead.

Amadu warned Graham what it was all about. "The labourers say they want more money. Massa say no." Amadu was calm and firm, a pillar of strength behind

87

my cousin. Always ready to see that he was not hum-
bugged, and always arranging things so that his master
should be in no danger of losing face.

The problem had to be faced, and Graham came out
to talk to the men. Amadu was standing respectfully a
little behind him. It was a difficult situation, for if our
carriers demanded their money and left us we should in
future have to find carriers from village to village, who
would have to be paid every day. In that case we would
not have enough money with us to get us more than
half-way to the coast. We had money waiting for us there.

I sat apart and watched. I could not hear what was
going on, but it lasted a long time. With their very few
words of English, and with Mark as interpreter, our
carriers were growling and muttering at Graham. He
looked calm, but some of his gestures were nervous.
The argument went on and on. Suddenly I could see
him decide to take a new line. He was going to bluff.
He waved his hand. All right, he seemed to say, go
home. Come for your money later and then go away.
And he turned as if everything were now at an end.

There was a moment's pause, and sudden sheepish
grins spread over the faces of our men. That was going
too far. They did not want to leave us. They were just
a lot of children trying to get something out of us. A few
of them had suggested it was worth trying, and the rest
had followed. But it had not worked, so it was all over
now; and smiling and laughing they forgot the whole
argument and were as friendly as ever. The only change
was that Graham went up in their estimation. For two
or three days they tried a few more irritating tricks, but

after that they gave them up, and we became again a big family party.

It was the right moment for a magnanimous gesture, and Graham told them they could kill the goat for their supper. They did so immediately, on the spot, right in front of my eyes and with no great skill. The hot, red blood spread out on the dusty ground, and I rushed into my hut wondering why I did not feel sick at the sight of it. It was just too hot to be emotional.

The carriers were in high good humour. Like children, they felt neither the future or the past. It was only the moment that counted. They had a goat for supper, so life was rosy. They laughed and danced, and we watched them and felt very happy that they had decided to stay with us.

My cousin rushed on with some of the carriers next morning; hurrying out of the village before he could get involved in any more discussions or requests from the carriers. I followed with every one else as soon as I was ready.

The forest seemed as dreary as it had been the day before, and I found it difficult to keep my mind occupied. But the men were in a merry mood and seemed to be making all kinds of jokes as we walked on.

Every now and then another path would lead out of ours to some village lying deep and invisible in the bush. The carriers with my cousin would lay a little branch across the path we were not to go down, to show my carriers the right way. It seemed to be their usual method, and until that morning it had worked admirably. But now for some reason, perhaps they were hurrying too much, or perhaps through the fault of my men, something went wrong.

I walked on with the boys and the carriers for many hours. The track seemed rougher than we had ever known it. Great trunks of trees had fallen across it, and big wild plants got in our way. We scrambled on, and at last came to a deserted village in an old clearing.

It was an eerie sight. Most of the houses had fallen almost into ruins, but a few were standing more or less complete. I wondered why it had been deserted. Had there been a fight, or had some horrid disease emptied this village of human life? It was not a pleasant place to linger in, but I wandered over to the far side of the clearing and stood under the trees for a rest and a drink.

I looked at my watch, which had decided to go that morning, and saw that it was past our usual lunch hour. I did not worry, for it was more than probable that Graham's watch was not going and that he would only stop to eat when he was really hungry. As he was not feeling well, I felt that that happy hour might not come for a very long time yet.

We went on. The way became so narrow and so rough that I could not understand how my cousin and his men had managed to slip through and leave so little trace of their passage. Laminah and Mark went on ahead with their swords cutting off big branches. Our progress was slow. The men with their heavy weights on their heads had to bend down to get underneath the boughs, and at the same time to climb over rotting tree-trunks. Finally the path simply died on us, and we were left facing a thick, impenetrable wall of jungle. It stood deep and solid in front of us.

We stood there, huddled together on the jagged thread of path, while I thought—this is a moment to think quickly. I could, of course, do nothing of the kind. Like ton weights one thought after another dropped heavily into my mind. Obviously we had lost Graham, and obviously it was going to be extremely difficult to find him again. I was the lucky one, for I had everything with me. I had most of the men, the money, the food, the beds, the mosquito-nets, the quinine—in fact, everything. Come what may, I should be all right. But I must search for Graham. However hard I racked my brain I could not remember the name of the village we were aiming at, and the men had forgotten it too. It began with B, but that was not enough to be of any use. The name of the village we had come from, of course, I had never known, but probably the men would be able to find their way back there. Would Graham turn back when he realised that we were lost, or would he go on and wait for us?

Strangely enough I was not in the least worried. I had grown so stolid of late, so phlegmatic, and I simply decided that it would be a waste of precious energy to fuss till I was quite sure that my cousin had disappeared for ever. It was very bad luck on him, for he was not well, and I wished, at any rate, that he had had the quinine with him, and his mosquito-nets. The scales had been unevenly balanced, and I had all the luck.

The men were getting restless and gave me nasty looks. "We go back," I said firmly.

Actually there was nothing else we could do, with that wall of African bush staring us in the face. If only I could remember the name of the village. I could remember Jbaiay, the name of the village we did not go to, but the other—a far simpler name—had completely slipped my memory. I was determined not to let the men see that I was puzzled. If I found as we were walking that I still could not remember it, we would go back to the last place.

"Missis say go back," said Laminah to Mark, and Mark shouted out something in a native dialect.

The men growled, and the headman slowly made his way towards me, pushed on by the others. He made some sort of a speech, which was heartily encouraged by the carriers, but of which I understood nothing except the words I had been expecting, "Too far."

The man with the money-box was standing beside me and seemed to be on my side, which gave me infinite confidence. Actually I was feeling amused at the whole situation—such a ludicrous huddle of humanity, such a chattering, in so many different dialects, like the tower of Babel—and my brain was incapable of taking in the seriousness of the situation.

I smiled sweetly at the headman. "I go on," I said. "And now for heaven's sake, shut up." He did not understand, but he smiled back his vague, pleasant smile, and shook his rattles rhythmically in his hand. The men were sitting along the path in a row on their cases, grumbling.

I turned on my heel and walked down the narrow path with the boys and some of the men. I did not look back, but presently I heard the rattles of the headman following me, and I decided the other carriers had made up their minds to come too. After all, they would be very foolish to go on sitting in the middle of the forest.

We passed through the deserted village, and I racked my brain trying to think of the name I had forgotten. Every now and then we gave a shout in case Graham should be within hearing distance. Suddenly out of the blue and in the nick of time a ragged old man appeared on the path. In his hand he carried a clump of bananas, and as I saw them the name of the village flashed through my mind. Bamakama! The nick of time! Dear old "nick," how I had always loved him. In wild-west films, appearing at the last second to save the heroine and kill the villain. And now here, in the centre of the African bush, he appeared again, in perfect film technique, in the guise of an old ragged man. What he was doing I cannot imagine, but he seemed very ready to help us. He knew Bamakama very well, and would take us a short cut to get there.

With one of those sensational changes of mood that still filled me with amazement, the carriers were now wildly excited. They sang, they danced, and they laughed. And every few moments we would yell all together in the vague hope that the others would hear us. It was certainly a strange way that the old man took us. With a sure instinct of direction, or else a real knowledge of the paths of the forest, he ran ahead, the green and yellow bananas in his arms, on his bare, flat feet. Down little, tortuous ways, crossing larger paths, over streams, like a bloodhound with his nose on the scent, never hesitating, never stopping.

As I followed I realised the chief reason why I felt so little upset at the situation I now found myself in. I was revelling in the relief from the boredom of walking without excitement. Trekking to-day had been an adventure. Circumstances were providing me with plenty to think about. The shouting every few moments was something new, and consequently interesting out of all proportion. Our voices did not echo through the forest; they were thrown back to us like the light of lamps in a fog.

I was just beginning to long for food when we came to a big broad river. We gave another shout, thinking that this time it would be carried along the water, when it was answered immediately.

There, on the other side of the river, sat my cousin and his men, waving their arms excitedly. Even Amadu allowed himself to show some feelings for once, for his relief knew no bounds. Of course, I should have been greatly relieved too, but it seemed to me a very tame ending to all our excitements. Life once again had been able to stage nothing better than an anti-climax. The saint that I had felt looked after the fools of the world was keeping too close a watch on us. It was a ridiculous situation. To happen to run across one another in that great forest as if it had been a village street.

We sat down by the side of the big St. Paul River, which we had crossed on a flat raft, pulling ourselves over by a rope made of creepers, and ate our lunch. It was beautiful. The slow, broad river, with its luxuriant green trees hanging over it. But its beauty was lost on me, and I only remembered it afterwards. I was feeling cheated, and too much looked after. Nothing exciting would ever happen, for something would always guard me. I was being too much cared for, like the baby of a large family. We still had quite a long walk before us, and suddenly we left the trees behind, and got into thick elephant grass. Finally we reached Bamakama.

There was an old rest-house there for travellers, but it was obvious that no traveller had passed there for many a long day, for the place was falling into ruins. The walls were covered in bugs and all kinds of creepy insects. Even our little monkey put his wizened old man's face between his hands, and moaned like a child. We had some tea to revive ourselves, and a swarm of flies descended upon us, covering our faces, our hands and our food. I struck out at them, snapping out all the curses I could think of, but they had settled for good, and we were forced to abandon our tea. We could hear our carriers muttering. They were having a palaver about who was to carry the water from the river for us. Also they did not like the second headman, who was a Mandingo.

Already the bugs had got into my clothes, and I occupied myself in trying to catch them. Graham, I noticed, was coming out in boils. I was not surprised. Our cook had made some strange white stuff that he said we were to eat to save our biscuits, for we were already running short of them. They were like dumplings, but far more solid. He called it bread, and we ate it with golden syrup.

"There is only one thing to do here," said Graham. "Get drunk."

By the time he had to go out to settle the men's quarrel he was feeling less pessimistic. The quarrel had turned into a tribal dispute, and the different tribes were grouped together, the one Mandingo was standing alone, hated by the others.

In his new mood Graham went out. He listened majestically for a few minutes. Then he gave his verdict firmly, prompted, I suppose, by the faithful Amadu, and lifting up his hand he said, "Palaver finished." Then (swaying, oh so slightly) he walked away. It was a superb performance. We were all astonished. The men had no more to say.

I did not drink whisky. I had found out already that instead of making me sleepy, it had the effect of keeping me awake, and I wanted to enter the realms of unconsciousness as quickly as I possibly could in this bug-ridden house.

The rest-house stood away from the village, so we were cut off from our usual evening amusements. Our carriers wandered down to join in the dancing, but we were very tired, and I crept early into my hard camp-bed. The smell in the house was terrible, and I could only suppose that a dead rat was lying about somewhere. Rats were running about almost before I got into bed, but they no longer troubled me. My whole body was swelling up in large red bumps, and all my clothes were so full of bugs that I knew that it would be impossible to get rid of them again.

I went to sleep.

# CHAPTER VII

WE were making now for Ganta and were walking
across a corner of French Guinea to avoid a big
détour. With a dreamlike inconsequence we would aim
first for one village, then for another, always hoping that
we were pointing our footsteps in the right direction.
Sometimes having definitely thought that we were
walking towards some particular place, it would suddenly
disappear. A mere mirage, a name we would never hear
again. Or else it would remain for days always just round
the corner, a will-o'-the-wisp, beckoning a mischievous
finger and saying, "Hurry up, try and catch me. Come
close or I will run away again!"

From the beginning of the trip we had heard of Ganta,
for it was a mission station, and the missionary, Dr.
Harley, was reputed to be a wise man and very knowledgeable about the secret societies and superstitions of
Liberia. But it was difficult for us to find. Nearly everywhere the name was unknown, for each little village is a
separate community, and though the villagers may
occasionally wander to the next village, they very rarely
leave their own tribes. But every now and then we would
hear the name, usually from a Mandingo trader, and
know that though we never seemed to get any nearer
to it, we were on the right road. Sometimes we were

told it was quite close by, but when we asked again it was suddenly a week's walk away. This uncertain element made our whole adventure as unsubstantial as a shadow, and gave it the magic quality of a fairy tale. It seemed such luck when we actually arrived at some place that we had been aiming at, that I could scarcely believe my eyes even when I saw it stretched out before me. I could never really understand how we had managed to get there.

The chief at Bamakama knew the direction of Ganta, and said that he would guide us as far as Galaye. He strapped on a sword and shot off with my cousin as early as possible next morning, before the carriers had time to think out any excuse for not going on.

It was only a short walk of three hours, and we arrived before the heat of the day had begun. The village was clean, and my hut stood right in the middle of it, which pleased me. The women were very much made up, with streaks of white paint smeared across their faces and their bodies. This was usually done for the sake of beauty, but it was considered a helpful medicine as well. A dash of paint on the forehead would cure a headache, or a dab on the stomach would help to ease them during their confinements.

To my delight the women brought me large paiis of steaming hot water, and I was told that it was the custom of the village to do this for strangers. I was very excited, and did not dream of asking if it had been boiled. I was determined to wash in that water even if it were swarming with guinea worms. Nothing would have made me give it up now that the temptation had been dangled before me. The tin bath was full almost to the top, and I soaped and splashed with enormous pleasure. As I was dressing afterwards, some of the women came in to take away the dirty water, but then decided to stay and watch me dress. I gave them a little pocket mirror in return for the hot water, but I could not make them understand what it was. I held it in front of one of them, pointed to her, and then pointed to the glass. It meant nothing to her at all, but it established a bond between us. Two minutes later I found that I had lost my only other mirror, but it seemed ungracious to ask for my present back again, so I let it go and did without one for the rest of the trip.

As the moon came up the dancing began. It was for moments like these that the trip was so worth while. The rats, the disease, the bugs, the jiggers, the little ants that fastened themselves on to one's skin in the forest, the stupefying boredom, the utter weariness one sometimes felt, the monotony of the food, and all the silly little daily irritations one got used to. But the beauty of the villages, the courtesy of the natives, the music, the dancing, the warm moonlit nights were things that gladdened the heart anew every day.

One girl pushed the others aside and danced alone, absorbed in what she was doing. Someone put a funny hat on her head. Every one laughed, but she did not seem to notice and continued to dance, wildly and fiercely. She was popular, for at the end every one crowded round her to show their approval by stroking her arms. The moon was getting into their blood. Even Amadu felt it, and thrusting the others aside, he lost his reserve and danced a spirited kind of war dance of his own country.

I was glad to see that it won admiration, for I felt rather like a mother showing off her child. He had been good to us and I wanted so desperately that he should do well before all these strangers. He gave one final leap, and the dance ended abruptly. Amadu moved to the back of the crowd. His face resumed its usual lines, his head came forward with its air of servile dignity and he became the perfect servant once more.

Next morning Graham rushed on ahead at a tremendous pace, for there was thunder in the air and murmurs among the men. A little boy became rather distressingly attached to me before we started. He had smallpox, and insisted on clinging to my shorts and running along beside me, looking at me with large, adoring eyes. Even Laminah appeared to think it was rather a pleasing sight, and I seemed to be the only one incapable of appreciating its æsthetic appeal.

On with the march.

We left the high elephant grass and plunged back into the forest. But this time the path was broad and the sun beat down on to our heads. When we stopped for lunch our boys hacked out a little clearing in the bush for us with their swords, so that for a little while we could enjoy some shade. During the rest of the day we had no protection at all from the glare.

We seemed to be off the path again. At least, when we set off in the morning Graham had told me that we should be spending the night in a place called Bamou. But Bamou seemed to have got mislaid, and we never found out the name of the village we did arrive in finally. I felt like the half-witted child I had once seen somewhere. It had a large notice tied round its neck on which was written in big letters, "I want to get to such and such an address in London." Every one was helpful as possible, the child was pushed about in various directions, and I felt quite sure that it would arrive safely eventually. We, too, equally helpless, I felt would arrive safely one day.

Our village was a disappointing place, for the chief was inhospitable and surly. He refused to cook any food for the men, and took us to a rest-house well outside the village. It was an unattractive hovel, consisting of one room, with a wooden verandah running round outside. That was all we could have for ourselves and thirty men, and our carriers were given strict orders that they were not to go down to the village that night. When darkness came the men rolled themselves up into their blankets and slept, packed closely together on the verandah. Their gentle snoring seemed like a strong bulwark for us against the unfriendliness of the village.

But first there was a quarrel to settle. A complicated one, for one of the carriers had stolen an old tin from one of the others and had sold it in the last village for one penny. In spite of the fact that we had plenty of old tins, the man who had been robbed demanded two shillings in recompense. It seemed to be a matter of honour in a way that was hard for us to understand. The thunder was rumbling in the distance and it was difficult to concentrate very much. Luckily at the height of the palavar there was a slight diversion, for we heard a wheezy bugle-call nearby, and could see a little procession winding up the road towards us. The quarrel was quite forgotten while we waited to see what was happening.

Suddenly everything turned into musical comedy. This I judged must be the rehearsal only of the real thing; otherwise I was sure the procession would now be singing the theme song. A boy led the way, blowing the bugle. Even the bugle had to be funny, so it gave out strange moans like a sick cow. A very old man followed, desperately overacting his part, it seemed to me, for he was walking with exaggerated weariness and carried over his shoulder an old gun—so old that little bits fell off from time to time. Then, surrounded by the gentlemen of the chorus, clad in suitable rags, a hammock with little curtains all round it was carried in. I naturally had no programme, but my theatrical sense told me that a sort of Bobby Howes would be inside it. I was right. The curtains were flicked aside and there—I could really almost believe it—sat Bobby Howes, disguised as a black chief. Out he jumped in his inimitable, agile way, and ran up to our house with little mincing steps, a comic dog at his heels. His costume, I felt, was a trifle overdone. His hair was arranged in little spiral curls, on the top of which balanced a minute topee, and he had put on fierce black whiskers. He also wore thick, black breeches, no stockings, but little white-kid boots and spats. In his hand he carried a long whip, which he brandished wildly; but as I was sure by this time that it really must be Bobby Howes, I had no fear of the whip. It was all just part of the fun. He made a long and elaborate speech in some strange dialect. It went on and on and on, and he hardly paused to draw breath. I got a little tired in the middle, and sat down on my chair. At last it was over, and Mark laconically translated the whole speech in six simple words. "Chief say go visit him to-morrow." We accepted, and the little man turned round and almost, but not quite, doing a step dance, popped back into the hammock and was carried off. As the musical comedy was apparently to be staged in the grand manner, there was an immediate burst of thunder, lightning flashed, and the tropical storm burst in the manner one has been brought up to expect at Drury Lane. It was a promising opening.

Scene two was set in Djiecke, the village of the chief, the time—much to our surprise—nine a.m. the following morning, for it had only taken us three hours to walk there.

Bobby Howes had changed into native dress, and the scene was laid inside his hut. I felt I ought to be singing some sort of song as I entered with Graham. I was obviously playing my part badly, but after all, I thought wildly, it's not every day one is expected to play lead at a moment's notice.

The chief sat at the far end, surrounded by his wives and daughters. The hut was full of them, and gingerly Graham and I picked our way through the heaps of semi-naked bodies. A little room was made for us and we sat down.

In the unexpected way in which things happen behind the footlights, the chief produced a bottle of French white wine.

"Oh, dear," I thought for a moment. "It's a pity they always exaggerate so on the stage. It's not quite the thing one expects to find in the middle of Africa." But then I remembered that I was in the middle of Africa, and that the chief was not really Bobby Howes. "It's all too difficult," my thoughts continued. "I had better just let things happen."

Some of the wives were good-looking and the daughters were lovely. They were lying in each other's arms, or sprawling over the chief, who brushed them off from time to time, good-naturedly, as if they were flies. Some of them were playing with a tame white rat, throwing it to each other, or letting it run about hither and thither over their bare bodies.

The chief—or Bobby Howes, whichever it was—filled up an old enamel mug with wine. He drank generously, and after refilling it passed it on to Graham. Then it was my turn. The wine was sweet, but quite pleasant, and the mug circulated rapidly between the three of us. At first I tried to find some spot to drink from that the lips of the chief had not touched, but I had to give it up. He had a peculiar way of drinking that ended up in a kind of lick round the edge of the mug, lapping up every stray drop. It was not the moment to be fussy, I felt. Soon our new friend was shining with the light of tremendous vitality, whipping up the spirits of every one in the hut, pressing cigarettes upon us, enjoying himself with extravagant abandon.

We soon finished the bottle and were all in a pleasant haze. By this time I hardly knew what was real and what was not. The hut seemed to be fuller than ever of bare arms, legs, breasts, and rats. We could not talk to the chief, but a charming daughter lay in his arms who, for some reason, could speak a few words of English. She was small and delicately made, and laughed incessantly at everything—at her father, at Graham, at myself, prettily and lightly, as she did everything else.

There was a moment's pause. It was our turn to return hospitality. We only possessed whisky, but as the chief was waiting for something, we sent for that. He put it in front of him and filled up the mug. This time he gave some to a few of his wives, who drank and passed the mug to the little daughter. She loved it, lapped it up with enjoyment, and laughed more than ever. Then we all drank, taking a sip in turn and passing on the old tin mug, laughing and wiping the sweat off our faces. The chief said something to his daughter.

"My fadder says you very fine woman," said the daughter to me, and we all laughed.

The wives were leaning back on one another, laughing with the chief and giggling at Graham. The chief gaped at me, watched me with staring eyes. The moment had come, I could not help thinking, when he should burst into romantic song. One could hardly carry on with this scene without music.

"My fadder says you very fine woman," said the girl again and again, in the same voice, like a broken gramophone record.

The hut was hot and stuffy, filled with the scent of black bodies, and almost overpowering in its atmosphere of sex and drunkenness. The chief was wearing some magnificent rings and bracelets. Without much hope I rather wished he would give me a few.

"My fadder says you very fine woman."

"I wish she'd stop saying that," I thought. "It sounds silly without music." The whisky was nearly finished. The wives were giggling, shaking like jellies with uncontrollable laughter. The white rat was forgotten and was running madly over every one. The little daughter was beginning to get sleepy. The scene was getting out of hand, I felt. The producer must have gone out to lunch and forgotten us. The chief was getting tired too, and no longer looked like Bobby Howes. His head rolled from side to side. His mouth was open and he dribbled a little bit from one corner. It was completely airless in the hut.

It was the right moment to take our departure. The whole thing suddenly sprang to life and became real, and it was obvious that I was going to get neither rings nor bracelets. The chief seemed ready to buy me from Graham, but we did not stay to hear what I was worth. I was tired of it all now, and ready to go.

The chief, with increasing hospitality, begged us to stay on. He almost wept with anguish as he saw us get up. The daughter seemed to be feeling a little sick as she stood up. She swayed and closed her eyes from time to time, as if the effort of keeping them open was a little too much for her. She was as pretty as ever, as charming and neat in her drunkenness as she had been when sober.

The chief tried to stand up. Several times he nearly managed it, but always he slipped down at the last moment. At last two strong men came to support him, and he staggered out of the hut, begging us to stay on. If I had not felt that I had really had enough of it all, he would have made me feel quite ashamed of myself. Two tactless people leaving too early, breaking up the whole party, upsetting the host.

"My fadder says you very fine woman," said the little daughter for the last time. She had suddenly changed her clothes, for she had heard that we wanted to take a photograph of her. She stood looking at us blissfully, with a kind of strange turban arrangement on her head which kept slipping over one eye.

We crept out of the village. The chief stood leaning against the side of the hut, wailing and whining, while the daughter, with her eyes closed, swayed gently backwards and forwards.

It was midday, and walking in the glimmering heat immediately after drinking alcohol was a strange feeling. It was not unpleasant, and prevented me from experiencing the usual deadening feeling of boredom. My head felt too heavy, but the rest of me floated along very pleasantly. My feet seemed hardly to touch the ground, like flying in one's dreams. I just drifted along gently and peacefully. I was ready to go on for hours. We left the thick, dead bush behind us again, and came out on to a plain of high elephant grass. The air was quivering in the heat, and there was a golden light over everything. Even the greyish-green of the elephant grass was glowing in deep rich tones. I floated on, thinking whatever idle thoughts happened to drift in and out of my mind.

We stopped for lunch. We had been getting bad food lately, for we had not brought enough tinned stuff with us and were living as much as possible on the produce of the villages we passed through. That meant rice, stringy chickens, and five or six eggs a day. The chickens had to be cooked and eaten immediately after they had been killed, and it was like eating lumps of rubber. One could chew and chew on the same piece for ten minutes or a quarter of an hour, but nothing could make it softer or easier to swallow. It was also completely tasteless.

The rice I liked, and the cook cooked it well, but meals were not times to look forward to with great excitement. Oranges were not grown in that district and we had seen no limes for a long time. So we had had no fresh fruit for many days and we began to need it badly. Graham did not feel well. He would put spoonfuls of Epsom salts into his tea both morning and evening, but they seemed to have no effect on him at all. Yet all the time he was hungry. As he walked along he would dream of heavy, spodgy food like steak-and-kidney pudding, and could eat with relish the heavy lumps of dough the cook called bread.

We both developed a startling love of sweet things. We had in our food boxes several tins of golden syrup. At the beginning we had not touched it, for we disliked its excessive sweetness, but now we were eating it by the spoonful. We had to ration ourselves, for otherwise we could easily have finished a tin at one sitting. Our tinned vegetables were running short too, and we began to economise as much as we could. We had a number of tinned turnips which we had not opened so far, as we both disliked turnips very much. But now we were forced to eat them nearly every day. No. Meals were not times to look forward to with pleasure.

Thunder was still in the air, and a little stab of fear pricked my heart like a red-hot needle. The rainy season was coming on unusually early that year. Although we had so far had only isolated storms, they were a warning to us that we had not much time to waste. The centre of Liberia at the foot of the hills is one big plain. For several months of the year it is nothing but a vast swamp; roads would be impassable and the hammock bridges would be swept away, and we might get caught in some village like wasps in the marmalade.

We came to the broad St. John River, slowly and heavily winding its way to the coast. The rivers of Liberia are apparently useless for navigation purposes, for they are said to be dangerous with endless falls and rapids. No one has yet traced them the whole way up to their source in French Guinea, and they flow darkly through the wildest, most unknown parts of the country.

"Back in our own land!" cried Mark joyfully, and the spirits of our carriers rose. For some odd reason it seemed to make them happy. We had certainly not expected this display of patriotic feeling, for they were still far from their own tribes. Perhaps it was just Mark's enthusiasm that spurred them on, or perhaps they were just in a good mood, for soon they started singing and ran along at twice their usual speed.

Unfortunately, after a little while their excitement died down, for they learnt that they were in the Manos district, where cannibalism as a religious ritual has never been stamped out. They were afraid. The victims of cannibalism are never members of the Manos tribe. They prefer to make use of strangers passing through.

And quite suddenly, after having tried to locate the place for days, we were in Ganta. We walked slowly up a long winding path, for we were very tired, and entered the village. It was a large place, surrounded by leopard traps: strange, primitive cages made of wood. Inside the trap the natives would place lumps of meat, and the leopard, once caught inside, would be unable to get out, for a little door would snap down over the opening.

The village straggled over the hillside, and we were surprised to see some little open-air stores, the first we had seen in Liberia. There were soldiers standing about, and Mandingo traders, and half-castes in European clothes. The compound of the District Commissioner was at one end of the village, while over a mile farther down the road was the little group of buildings that belonged to the mission. Between the two the village spread out untidily and forlornly.

We walked up to the village and were welcomed by Dr. Harley.

# CHAPTER VIII

THERE was something wrong. I could feel it immediately. We should not have come on that day. How I knew this with such certainty I could not tell, but I felt it. Deep down in my heart I knew we were trespassing on sacred ground, and I wished we were far away, anywhere, but not in Ganta.

Dr. Harley welcomed us gently, looking at us unsmilingly with his deep, mournful eyes. His wife, in a white dress, with a face like chalk, seemed almost too ethereal for this world. She was thin, with deep shadows under her eyes. A woman, all soul and no flesh. She hardly ever spoke. After asking us in a whisper to join them at supper that evening, she relapsed into silence and became just part of the spirit of the mission, no longer a human being. Fate, perhaps, or Tragedy. There was nobility in the light shining from her eyes. One had to keep looking at her to see if she was still there. Like the whisper of her voice, she could so easily fade away. Her soul would remain, but her body, the most unreal thing about her, might disappear. It was difficult even to remember what she looked like if one was not actually looking at her. I began to wonder if she were really there, or if I was the only one that was seeing an apparition.

Two little white-faced boys walked about hand-in-hand. Dear little things, but thin and listless. Too tired to talk or play, they kept as near to each other as they could, and watched us with big, solemn eyes.

And during supper, over us all there lay a feeling of sadness. The memory of the two older people was bringing a guest to supper that we could not see. And into all our minds deep, melancholy thoughts came and settled. Doors that had been locked for a long time were opened, and sad little pictures of the past came back with an air of pathetic loneliness. I could not know who their invisible guest was. I did not know then that there had once been three white-faced little boys wandering round the mission and that one of them had died. Or that we had arrived on the first anniversary of the child's death, and that his little grave was standing outside the door, where they could see it every time that they left the house. I did not understand these things, but I felt that I wanted to take the brittle fingers of the little white woman in mine and comfort her. But I knew that I could bring her no comfort. I was only a stranger passing through. It brought no pleasure to her to have the loneliness broken for a day or two. I was only a burden to her that had to be borne, like the many, many other burdens that lay on her shoulders.

After supper Dr. Harley talked to us, putting aside his private sorrows and playing, gallantly, the part of host. Every now and then his head would sink down between his hands in an effort to remember what he was talking about. And sometimes he would get up quickly and open the door to see if anyone were listening. They were after him, he said. His boys thought that he knew too much. One day they would kill him. He expected it all the time . . .

just a little poison in the food . . . a sudden stab in the dark. Soon they would get him. And he brushed his hand over his tired, world-weary eyes.

He talked of the unhealthiness of the country, and we remembered suddenly that we had forgotten to take our quinine for the last day or two. Great is the power of suggestion, and strange things may be achieved through its strength, for as he spoke he looked at me strangely, and before I remembered that I was really feeling extremely well—better actually, apart from mental weariness, than I ever did in England—I began suddenly to imagine that I was beginning a fever. My hands began to feel damp and my head hot. I shivered once or twice. I was on the verge of saying that I would like to go and lie down. My eyes seemed to burn. But then luckily I caught sight of myself in a mirror across the room, and at the sight of it I had to smile, for I looked the picture of health. Dirty, red-faced, unattractive perhaps, but not, certainly not, in the least weak or ailing.

The sombre voice of the doctor drifted back slowly into my consciousness.

"Did you ever drink palm wine?"

"Very occasionally," answered my cousin. "Not more than once or twice."

"The worst thing for dysentery."

He had been out in Ganta for seven years and he knew what the climate could do. He had just sent home a man, dead, who had walked up from Monrovia.

We asked how far it was to Sinoe, which was the place that Graham had decided that we should aim for. "Four weeks," said Dr. Harley, and our hearts sank within us.

Certainly I was very healthy, but Graham had already been rather sick for days. Another four weeks. Twenty-eight days of the endless boredom of walking through the forest hour after hour. If it had been a little earlier in the year, I could so happily have spent many weeks in one of the gay, happy villages we had passed through, but the pressing on, the race with the rains, was a horrifying thought. And Graham's pains? Could he stand another four weeks of early rising, bad food and rapid walking? The doctor told him that he had been walking too fast, too far, and without sufficient resting times. It was sheer madness in that climate.

I could see Graham wilting. When one is already far from well it is not the best time to hear tales of sickness and death.

We were rather subdued as we walked back to the rest-house that Dr. Harley had lent us. It was only a hundred yards from his own house. We walked past the little grave and saw everything glimmering in the moonlight. Whatever lay in the future for us, I was quite sure that it was all worth while. Without any doubt I would rather be out there than knitting a jumper, or going to some party or dinner in London. Never in Europe could I have found those moments of pure beauty and peace. Loveliness unspoiled.

A high tree with white flowers like camelias was rustling in the gentle breeze. The flowers caught the moonlight and they glowed slightly like dim lights. Far in the distance the everlasting harp was being played.

I sat by my window for hours that night while the rats ran round my room. There was nothing I could see: no dancing, no natives, just the edge of a wood. I was part of it somehow. It was no longer all one joke, a game that I had entered into impetuously. It meant something deeper and more valuable to me now. It was a precious thing to have had in my life.

We were descending now from the hills, and were at the beginning of the great plain, and already I could feel the difference. Even the nights were hot and sticky now. I kicked off all my bedclothes and tossed restlessly on my hard camp-bed. From now on the days would become ever hotter and damper, for Ganta was our turning-point and we would be walking south. We would experience the kind of weather that takes every drop of energy out of the body. We had known it hot the whole time, but now we would soon know it far hotter. It would be very damp, and there would be no long cool nights to repair our strength. It was beginning now, I could feel it already. My limbs felt like lead.

We stayed three days at Ganta. Every hour Dr. Harley worked like a slave, rushing to see patients in the bush, looking after natives in his surgery and his hospital, treating yaws, leprosy, craw-craw, smallpox, injecting between two and three hundred natives every week for venereal disease. Giving up his life and youth to this tremendous work, offering up everything he possessed, wearing out his nerves and health in this small lost corner of the world. Seven years he had been in Ganta, and now he was sick and tired in body and mind, in desperate need of a long holiday—suffering from persecution mania and expecting death every moment. He felt it waiting for him. He could not trust his boys. And every moment he could spare from his battle against disease he studied the secrets of the natives. One would tell something, another add some more. He had learnt the native dialect, and his patients in their agony would let out more strange things than they realised. Slowly, slowly, year in and year out, he had listened and noted, sifted the truth from the falsehoods, learnt and waited, till gradually he understood more than anyone in the world of the native life of that district. But in the process he had become unbearably tired. He was wearing out his brain till at times he looked, and felt, a little mad. He never rested. It was work, work, work, all day, and in the evening it began again. Work, work, work. While his boys spied on him and tried to find out how much he really knew of the native secrets.

During one evening, in the dusk when the light was dim and sombre, he took us to a room that he kept locked up. Looking over his shoulder to make sure that no one was about, he slipped in, and we followed. All round us we saw strange masks of every kind. Cruel faces grinned at us, and others, ugly and grotesque, seemed almost alive. We were surrounded by them, and they were all hideous, though carved with great skill. He had collected them ever since he had first come out. Some of them were dangerous for him to have in his possession, for they belonged to the women's societies. One I saw was not intended for the eyes of women. It was a wicked thing, roughly carved, but strong and evil in expression. I could find no beauty in any of them, but they were certainly a valuable and unique collection. He would not tell us where he had found them, or how he had obtained them, though he said that one or two of them had been given him by grateful patients. When he had first arrived in Ganta, he made no secret of his interest, but now he had learnt better. Sometimes he could hear his boys whispering. He had learnt their language and could understand what they said. There were many things that it would be better for a white man in the bush not to know. Mrs. Harley flitted round silently like a pale moth. She moved with a lovely grace, whispering gentle words whenever she saw us. She helped her husband in the surgery, mixing the medicines and acting as nurse, she looked after and taught her children, and she ran the house. But her greatest joy was her garden. She had taught the wilderness to blossom like the rose, and her flowerbeds were a blaze of blooms. She also took endless trouble with her vegetables, and whenever we had a meal at her house we ate all kinds of exotic and strange things that tasted to us like food for the gods.

There were so many things that we wanted to ask Dr. Harley, but we had to let him choose his own time. Sometimes he was working too hard. Sometimes he was too tired. At other times he felt too nervous. He told us that he would come over to our rest-house one day, where his boys could not spy on him, and that there he would talk to us.

In the meantime Laminah had toothache. One could always count on Laminah to bring things down to the ridiculous. Ever since we had arrived in Ganta he had walked round with a drawn sword, expecting to find a horde of cannibals waiting for him behind every bush. But now he sat by himself on the steps of our house, with his cheek in his hands, putting up a superb performance of a creature in agonising pain and demanding endless sympathy from every one. We handed him over to the doctor, and in a few minutes the most blood-curdling yells and screams issued from the surgery. The offending tooth was being pulled out, but it would have been easier to imagine that he was slowly being tortured to death by Dr. Harley. After the operation he was something of a hero with the other men, but for many days he was scared to death, and would sit crouching in some dark corner, shivering with fright, his little woollen cap on his head, and looking somehow exactly like our monkey.

I found some old magazines during one afternoon and lay down and tried to read. I was unable to concentrate on a single word, and instead spent hours gazing, with the greatest interest, at all the food advertisements. Cool-looking asparagus tips, tomato-juice cocktails, pink luscious Virginia hams. Chocolates of all sorts and shapes in expensive-looking boxes. And almost the most satisfying picture of all—a large glass of bubbling Eno's Fruit Salts. I turned over the pages slowly, revelling in each picture, greedily remembering past meals and eagerly planning future ones. I could not get much variety in my plans for there was only one thing that I was really wanting. I was longing for smoked salmon. Like the old man in *Treasure Island*, who, deserted and left alone on an island in the middle of the ocean to die, had dreamt throughout the years of cheese, just cheese. So I for the rest of the trip yearned passionately for smoked salmon. Like the old man, I could almost see it before my eyes, but it vanished when I stretched out my hand. Graham had a little twitching nerve over his right eye. When he felt particularly unwell it would twitch incessantly, and I watched it with horror. It fascinated me, and I would find my eyes fixed upon it till I was almost unable to look anywhere else. I did not tell him about it, for I got to know it so well that I was able to gauge how he was feeling without having to ask him. Soon we would have to press on. We could, of course, go straight on to Monrovia from Ganta, but that would be too ignominious. It was the usual route and was taken by all travellers or missionaries to Ganta. It would be humiliating to descend to that. We had come to Liberia to keep off the beaten track and to walk through the unknown parts. But to trek to Sinoe was out of the question so far as we could see at the moment, and so it was better to try for Grand Bassa. We could start that way, and then if Graham got better, we could still branch off. The way to Grand Bassa would be primitive and interesting, but it would be shorter.

I was definitely frightened. In a day or two, I thought, we shall be away from Dr. Harley; I shall be alone with the twitching nerve, and I understood absolutely nothing about nursing. Graham too felt uncomfortable. Illness in the bush too often means death. And Graham, to his own surprise, found that he did not want to die. He discovered in himself an intense love of life. I watched him put spoonfuls of Epsom salts in his tea. His face was grey, and it was only his tremendous will-power that was giving him his burning vitality.

The afternoon was steaming hot. Half an hour before, I had changed my shirt, and already my fresh one felt damp and sticky. I had been writing in my diary and my hands were covered with the purple of my indelible pencil. I felt overpoweringly sleepy and was wondering whether I should lie down on my bed for a little while. In the distance I could hear the moans of Laminah, which by this time had become like the running accompaniment to the main theme of our daily life.

Dr. Harley slipped into the room. He looked carefully out of the window to see if anyone had followed him, opened the door again suddenly, sprang once more to the window, and then suddenly sat down. The great moment had come. The mysteries of the bush would be revealed to us. With the utmost generosity the doctor was spreading his knowledge at our feet, offering us the work of years. His tired eyes looked at us out of his thin, clever face—the face of an ascetic or a saint. A man who had given up his life to great and noble aims.

Life is full of bathos. The romantic moment is too often spoiled by an attack of hiccoughs or a slip on a banana skin. A great achievement can be turned into a joke by some little misprint in the papers. Or, as unfortunately in this case, a thrilling moment may be left hanging in the air by sheer weariness, until it falls flat and useless on the ground.

With all honesty I confess I was incapable of understanding nearly everything that Dr. Harley said to us. Sleepiness, so overpowering that it became an agony, crowded into my brain. I could listen to all he said, but two minutes later it was all forgotten. Weird things he told us, that for a few moments would make my hair stand on end with horror, but would then fade and leave but a shadow, a wraith of themselves behind—tales of cannibals of the district, for there was no doubt that cannibalistic rites were still carried out, and that in spite of the half-hearted efforts of the Government the human heart and the soft palms of the hands were still needed and used for secret religious festivals.

I am no anthropologist, and I could only think, with the same forgetfulness of good English as Alice in Wonderland, that everything was getting "curiouser and curiouser."

Times without number had I seen the village blacksmiths at work at their fires, but never had I guessed that almost invariably was he the local devil. These natives, who had been initiated under him in the bush schools would learn that the blacksmith, whom they had always known, was also the devil, but they would be sworn to secrecy. They would continue to fear the devil when he wore the mask, but still be able to think of the blacksmith as a perfectly ordinary man who had always lived among them. A strange psychological frame of mind. It was as if the blacksmith were given two characters: his human one and a supernatural one which put him into the position of teacher and leader in the village. The women, too, had their devil. She, too, would be one of themselves, but never would the natives be able to connect the two characters in their minds. When they put on their masks they became a Thing, a Power, something that could remain there, watching even when it came back into human form, and went round performing the usual everyday things.

The doctor told us many tales of the Leopard Societies, and the Alligator Societies, strange, dark and horrible.

He went. And in less than two minutes I was fast asleep. So do Life's most interesting moments pass us by.

With deep shame I confess this. It would, perhaps, have been better if I had read up this subject before attempting to write this book, so that I would have something to offer to those who are yearning for knowledge, but I had decided to write a book of truth. And that is the bitter, humiliating truth. I had failed utterly and completely to profit by the teaching of this great man.

It was time to go on, to take to the road once more. I had no feeling whatsoever for the Romance of the Road. To me, in spite of all the poets who have sung its praises, it was a matter of complete boredom. I got no feeling of freedom. No deep thoughts came crowding into my mind, helping me to understand the meaning and purpose of life. Rather the opposite. I was very glad for any thoughts at all that would condescend to occupy my brain for a few moments. I was not even filled with any particular sensations of the joy of living, nor did I wish to sing that "the life of a tramp is the life for me." No. The day's march was the only method of getting from one place to another, and I would gladly have done it by car, if it had been possible to do so under the present circumstances.

The jungle too. Volumes have been written on the beauties of the jungle, and I can only suppose that they were very different to this one. Here it seemed dead, untidy, endlessly big but without any vitality. There was nothing but a ghastly monotony and dreariness. I would have been glad of some excitements, relieved if I had thought there was any possibility of danger.

We left in the early morning and Dr. Harley accompanied us. For years he had heard of a sacred waterfall, but had been unable to find it. An old pupil of his from the school in Ganta was now chief of a village near by and had at last promised to guide him there. Ganta looked like a cinema village as we passed through it in the early morning light. It lay spread out untidily and gave a flimsy impression, as if the huts were made of cardboard which would be removed next day to make room for the next set. I would not have been surprised to see Miss Dorothy Lamour strolling towards me in a brief but well-cut tiger skin, or to see some tawny Tarzan of the Apes striding off towards the forest for his next shot. Even our party, though perhaps too raggedly dressed, looked as if we were about to play some dramatic scene: the missionary, the blond young hero, and the girl.

We met the chief and climbed what the natives believe to be a holy hill. Little fairy people live on the hill, the chief told Dr. Harley, and from time to time gifts had to be brought to them and left in certain places.

The paths to the waterfall were thickly overgrown, for about fifteen years ago the natives had stopped offering human sacrifices to the snake that they thought lived in the waters, and the snake had departed and made its way to the St. John River.

It was a steep hill, and as we climbed I was preparing my mind for another anticlimax. All this mystery, this scrambling through the bush along an almost invisible path, this talk of fairies and holy hills, was no doubt magnificent showmanship, but what would it lead to? Probably some little pool and a small splash of water that only the most romantically minded traveller could get really thrilled with. For I was growing cautious, building up a defence within myself against disappointments.

I was far too stolid in my nature to be able to imagine beauties and excitements where my eye did not see them.

We moved slowly, for every foot of the way had presently to be cut with heavy cutlasses. All signs of a path had disappeared, and the chief and his men were relying on their sense of direction. Most of the way we were walking uphill, but suddenly we started going steeply down again.

All at once we could hear the sound of splashing water, and soon we could smell it too. The men hacked with all their strength and we scrambled after them.

We arrived at the bottom of the hill and found ourselves in a glade. A deep pool lay at our feet, and from sixty feet above our heads a magnificent waterfall came rushing down, catching the sunlight in a million brilliant colours, and ending in a snow-white froth of foam. Big rocks and boulders were clustered round, and were covered with luxuriant green moss and ferns. The glade filled with men, women, and children. They had apparently all come with us, but the bush had been so thick that we had noticed only those in our immediate vicinity. We stood and gazed. The water roared and the echo thundered round the boulders. The glade seemed alive; even the trees round were more colourful than any we had seen in the bush. It was a magnificent place for a sacrifice and as holy as an old temple.

I climbed to the top of the rock over the waterfall and watched the water rushing down below me. It was powerful and majestic, as if conscious of its own strength. The roar of the water was like a hymn of praise to heaven.

I was filled with an almost uncontrollable desire to push

someone over the edge into the whipped-up waters below. Just one little movement, one jerk of my arm, and away they would go.

I thought of the old sacrifices and the reason why they had stopped. Fifteen years ago the last victim must have been standing where I was standing at that moment. The glade must have been filled with people, singing and dancing. It was probably moonlight. The mythical snake was thought to be in the water waiting, smacking its lips for its meal of human flesh. The priest tied the hands of the victim behind him. The crowd watched. The priest was about to push the man over, when the man himself, with his hands tied behind his back, jumped into the waterfall, somehow pulling the priest in with him, hanging on to his robes with iron fingers. And so the snake had two human beings in his pool that night.

The priest had been an important man, a chief of four villages. He had died without naming his successor. For a long time there had been squabbles who was to be the next chief, and when it was finally settled, one year had passed by with no sacrifice to the snake. And the snake, dissatisfied and furious, had gone away.

We climbed the long way back, our legs aching with the effort, and got back once again on to our road. We said good-bye to Dr. Harley. I turned and watched him go down the road. From the back it looked like the figure of a very old man. He walked away surrounded by the boys he could not trust. Once he turned and waved. Then he disappeared.

We turned our faces south.

# CHAPTER IX

"I WISH he would pull up his socks," I said to myself, as we were striding along, for by this time I had got well into the way of talking to myself as if I were two people. I found it very entertaining. Never before had I suspected myself of invariably holding two completely opposite points of view on every subject that cropped up. "I do wish he'd pull up his socks. I don't mind anything else. Really nothing else in the world. But it looks silly to have one's socks hanging round one's ankles in that childish way. I can't bear it. Can't I ask him to pull them up? It wouldn't be much to ask. I would just say at lunch-time, 'Oh, Graham, do pull your socks up'——or would he think I was getting irritable and petty and touchy about little things? Or I could say quite casually, as if I were really thinking of other things, 'Funny, isn't it, the way your socks slip down?' Would he think of pulling them up after that? Shall I ask him why he lets them hang down like that?"

My other self answered. It was the more practical half of me, and had sharp, clear answers to everything. "Don't be a fool. There are only two things that he could possibly answer. Either he has lost his garters, or else, not realising the importance of the question, he'll say, 'My dear girl, what the hell does it matter?'"

Yes, I thought. There's nothing to be done. Every day I shall have to walk behind him. For the first quarter of an hour I shall watch his socks slipping slowly, so very slowly, over his calves and down to his ankles, and there they will lie, useless, in little round wrinkles, like an old concertina. It's too awful. I must put my mind on something else immediately, I thought firmly.

For the next quarter of an hour I was fairly happy. I had put my mind on smoked salmon.

We were clamouring downhill over rough paths and towards the thickest bush that covers the great plain in central Liberia. Graham was looking better, but though he was still striding on ahead, he was not keeping on at his usual pace. I was but a few yards behind him, and consequently it was the first time that I had noticed the sad behaviour of his socks.

It is foolish that it is always the little things that are so hard to bear, and I never realised that while I was doing my best to keep calm about the socks, Graham was beginning to find the shape and cut of my shorts almost more than he could stand. I was used to them by this time and had long ago given up feeling selfconscious in them, but to Graham they started at this stage to become more and more horrible every day.

Friday night may be "Amami" night in England, but when we arrived in Peyi it was quite definitely "delousing" night. All through the village little groups of women were sitting together picking away at each other's heads. The most popular "delouser" seemed to be a woman with particularly unhealthy-looking sores on her hands. She was as quick and neat at her job as a monkey.

It appeared to be a most absorbing occupation, for although we were in a district now where the natives had never before seen a white face, some of the women never stirred towards us till their heads had been finished.

It was a depressing village at first sight, for it seemed to be a village of the maimed and aged. Every one was diseased and the whole place looked distressingly poor. When the "delousing" operations were finally complete the natives crowded round our hut, and the women peeped in while I was washing. It was rather like having a bath in Trafalgar Square, but I no longer minded.

The chief was a man with little authority. He was sitting apart, all by himself, making a mat. When he had finished it, the others came to look at it. They seemed to admire it, for they took it away from him, and he was left alone again looking rather forlorn. He did his best to find food for our carriers, but it seemed impossible to find much, and he only succeeded in getting hold of one little bucket full of rice. To our surprise our men did not mind; they seemed to realise that it was a poor village and forgave the chief generously. The endless dissatisfactions and grumblings of the men seemed to be a thing of the past. Also it was the night of the full moon, and already the excitement was in their blood. Drums were being beaten, rattles shaken, and if anyone could find no other instrument, he would bang two sticks together rhythmically. As soon as it became dark the dancing began, and our carriers, and the sick, the old and the blind were moved to some joy that only Graham and I could not feel. We were outside this strange influence, this effect of the moon that was as heady as champagne.

All night they danced, and, "We were so happy last night," said Mark, next morning, to Graham. In spite of empty stomachs, they were still in a merry mood when we reached Sacrepie next day.

Sacrepie was a town of the Paramount Chief. It was big, and full of life and vitality. Soldiers of the Frontier Forces in strange pastel-coloured uniforms, and tall Mandingo traders with their heavy Semitic type of features, were wandering about. The huts were spread out over a large area. They were in good repair and the place looked prosperous and busy. Some of the Mandingos had spread their wares on the street, and little clusters of men were standing about, idly and good-naturedly haggling over prices.

The Paramount Chief was away, but we were met by his son, who wore a kind of Boy Scout hat and had the flustered and unrestful manner of ineffectual individuals who are over-anxious to please. He took us along to his father's compound and gave us a house. Then he sat on the verandah, perspiring with agitation, shaking with nervousness, and bothering us with his attentions. He wanted to give us presents, and ordered that someone should go and get them. But no one listened. They turned away and smiled. He felt that he had lost face before us, which increased his sense of inferiority and made him still more anxious to impress us.

A smooth and oily Mandingo in a red fez bowed before us, rubbing his hands and smiling a soft, ingratiating smile—a smile that somehow never managed to reach his eyes before it was suddenly turned off, as quickly as one might turn off the electric light.

"I will buy your chairs," he said, in excellent English. "I find them interesting. I will also buy your table."

"We are going to Monrovia," said Graham, in a rather surprised voice. "I'm afraid we shall still need them."

"I hope every one has been very kind to you in our country. I also like your beds."

"I'm afraid——" began Graham.

"My name is Steve Dunbar."

"Yes," said Graham, exactly as if he had expected it to be.

"Presently you will see elephants. Hundreds of them in the forest. They will be running about here and there. We have a very beautiful country. Do you not agree? And we are very hospitable people. We will do anything you like."

"We would like food for the men," we answered firmly. "And at once."

"Certainly." He turned to the chief, and after murmuring a few words, faced us once more. "The chief agrees."

Steve Dunbar seemed to be enjoying our conversation, for without any encouragement from us he went on: "You must go to Baplai. It is on your way. I have a friend at Baplai. He is a civilised man. You will like him *very* much. He is a civilised man."

"You know the way to Grand Bassa?" we asked.

"You must go first to Baplai, and there you will see my friend. And you will also see hundreds of elephants. Then you must go to Toweh Ta. Now I will go away, but I will see you again in Monrovia. I will meet you there and then I will buy your things. I find them interesting." And after going inside our house again to take one final look at our possessions, Steve Dunbar turned and walked out of our lives as unexpectedly as he had stepped into them a few moments ago.

Laminah as usual was shaking with fright. We must buy a goat at once. No, not to eat, but to keep the elephants away in the forest. Elephants, he explained as carefully and condescendingly as one explains some simple but well-known fact to a child, elephants do not like goats. If they smelt one they would immediately run away in fear and we would then be left in peace. Only a goat could save us. A very, very little goat would do. A baby goat— and he held his hands in front of him, indicating a goat about the size of six inches. He would try to find a cheap one.

We sat on the verandah and waited for the food for the men. It was still afternoon, but our men had had so little to eat the day before that we wanted them to have a meal as soon as possible.

There was a big space in front of our house, with a ring of huts all round it, which belonged to the fifty-five wives of the Paramount Chief. In the middle there was the usual clump of feathery-looking trees for the rice birds, which were supposed to bring luck to the village in spite of the fact that they damaged the crops year after year. The chief's son was still sitting with us, puffing and blowing, and still persisting in the attempt to try to make us believe him to be a man of importance in spite of all evidence to the contrary and our utter lack of interest. Every now and then he would dart off for a moment to give new instructions about our carriers' food. Apparently it was going to be a most magnificent feast, which pleased us, for it was forty-eight hours since they had had a square meal.

The cook, in robes that were beginning to lose their first virginal spotlessness, came running up to Graham. In one hand he held a chicken and the other he was waving wildly in the air. A torrent of words broke from his lips, and his eyes were wild and distrait. Graham looked completely bewildered, which was not surprising, as it was impossible to hear one word of what the cook was saying.

"No sabby," said my cousin, relapsing most un-expectedly from the kind of English he usually spoke into the English he vainly imagined that our boys used. The cook began again. It seemed to have something to do with the chicken, for he was shaking it with the greatest fury. But what it was all about we never clearly found out, for in a puzzled, cautious voice Graham said, "I agree," and the cook, with a beaming smile, was off to the cook-house like a flash of lightning. The time seemed to be passing in a series of unconnected scenes, like a trailer of next week's film.

There was a muttering of voices and the sound of drums, and over the high wall surrounding the compound stepped two devils on stilts twenty feet high. They wore high black hats and black masks, and the rest of their bodies were covered with pink-and-white-striped garments like pyjamas. The same material covered their stilts in such a way that they really looked like horribly thin, long legs.

They came swaying towards us, sometimes taking little running steps and flapping their arms, and sometimes with great strides. Then they pranced before us, either playing the fool like two clowns in a circus, or dancing with grace and elegance, as sophisticated as if they had been trained by Mr. Cochran for his next London revue. Their movements meant all or nothing according to the tastes and imaginations of their audience, and they had an air of experience that seemed strangely out of place. They had an excellent sense of timing their tricks. They would stand quite still for a long time till they were quite sure that we were all watching, and then slowly fall back, while we held our breath, thinking they must surely crash to the ground. Suddenly they would step back, recover their balance, and amble nonchalantly off to sit and rest on the roof of one of the houses, fanning themselves languidly with one hand. At last the show ended, they stepped back over the high wall, and walked off down the long dusty road that led to their own house.

Thunder was beginning to rumble. I did not like it. So often it seemed to make its appearance on our more dramatic moments. As I listened now, I got the feeling that all was not well with our little world.

The chief's son had brought one of his wives to see us. We asked him if the food was ready for our men, for it was getting dark and the carriers were gathering round waiting for it. The man indicated that it was coming. It was going to be a great feast, so it was taking time to prepare.

We had our supper. The sky was overcast and the air was heavy with moisture. There would be no moon.

We insisted on seeing the men's supper being cooked, and the chief seemed delighted to show us. He took us through the village. It was already night-time, and in each little hut we could see the small fires burning. The chief's son was whining weakly and was trying to ingratiate himself with us by putting on a stupid, pathetic air, pretending to be miserable because we were angry at his inefficiency and turning down the corners of his mouth like a foolish, spoilt child. He took us to a hut and showed us food, piles of it, being cooked by a woman of the village. We could not talk to her, but our headman who was with us seemed satisfied, although he too could not make himself understood.

We went to bed. Very, very late Amadu went in to Graham to tell him that no food had been prepared for the men, but that they had now gone off to sleep.

I dreamt that it was not I who had pushed someone off into the sacred waterfall, but that I myself had been pushed off. I woke up screaming, clutching the bedclothes, but the dream went on. The roar of the echoes was in my ears and the waters were splashing all round me. For a long time I could not sort out in my mind where the dream ended and reality began. I struggled and pushed the water away from my face. Gradually I realised that the storm had burst and the rains were descending with great force through the roof and on to my bed. I was soaking wet. I got out of my bed and put on another pair of pyjamas and my mackintosh, and sat shivering on my camp-chair for the rest of the night. Outside I could see the lightning flashing by in exciting yellow and green stripes.

In the morning the carriers came to us looking like a horde of drowned rats, but hungry and miserable as well. We comforted them as much as we could. We had with us a small store of rice for serious emergencies which the men now cooked for themselves, and we gave them some money to buy a goat, which so raised their spirits that they became almost gay. They did not seem to blame us. It was the chief's miserable son who had let us down, and Graham, with his instinctive and almost uncanny understanding of the psychology of the carriers, wanted to show them that he too thought the man a low-down wretch. He sent for him, and he came and stood in front of my cousin with the hang-dog expression of a weak man who knows he has done wrong but has no defence. Graham did not get up, and the carriers stood round in a ring. Slowly, with many biting expressions and in good round terms that no one except myself understood, Graham delivered his lecture. The effect on our men was miraculous. They loved it. It was as good as a show. I thoroughly enjoyed it myself.

But it was after nine-thirty before we could get off, and the paths were knee-deep in mud, particularly thick and glutinous mud. In some parts the carriers were wading nearly up to their waists in it, and we had to be carried either on the backs of one of them, or, whenever possible, in the hammock. By this time I no longer noticed their strange smell, and my only object was to avoid being carried either by the one with yaws or the one with venereal sores.

I began to get some idea now of what the country would look like in the rainy season. Here the villages were no longer standing grandly on the hill-tops, but were spread out on the plains, so that one came upon them suddenly in the forest. The paths would quickly become impassable, and the rivers would flood, till the whole plain would become one big, dismal marsh.

We had started late, so the heat of the day was on us from the beginning. It dried up the water on our paths, and a little mist rose up everywhere. The effect was soft and ghost-like and a little mysterious, but, it must be confessed, distinctly malodorous. We were right off the beaten track now, away from the paths of missionaries and gold and diamond prospectors. Up till now we had seen, from time to time, little holes dug in the bush, like neglected open graves—sad little signs that the Dutch prospectors had passed that way and found nothing. Now we were alone, and in passing would leave no trail behind us except, perhaps, an old tin or two.

Children screamed when they saw us, as if some frightening bogey man of their dreams had come to life. Even the women we met in the bush away from their homes would give a horrified moan and dart away into the forest. In the villages, of course, it was different, for there were plenty of them congregated together to give each other courage. There the natives screamed and yelled with excitement, cutting off big branches from the trees and running along beside us. Sometimes they would dance, and our carriers with them, doing quite complicated steps with the heavy weights on their heads. Once I joined in and they yelled with delight; all except Amadu, whose serious eyes silently reproached me for my lack of dignity. The natives would run with us out of their villages for about half a mile and then stop suddenly, as if they had come to the frontier of another land, and they would then stand in a row waving their branches. In one place the men of the village made me get into my hammock, and four strong men picked it up and rushed me round and round at a tremendous pace, shouting with joy, till Amadu and Laminah drew their swords and flew at the men with such a ferocious expression on their faces that they dropped my hammock and fled. "Uncivilised labourers," muttered the boys, in tones of fury and scorn.

We were to reach Baplai that afternoon, the home of Steve Dunbar's friend, Mr. Nelson, the civilised man. I was feeling curious, for it was only later that I found out that anyone in Liberia who has been to school for more than two months and can write his own name is entitled to call himself a civilised man. An honour that is paid for with a small yearly tax.

The villages were getting poorer and poorer. The huts looked tumbled-down and wretched. The natives, in spite of their high spirits, looked as if they were on the point of starvation. The men in the bush carried with them bows and arrows. The forest here was thicker than it had been, and sometimes the carriers would point out the marks of leopards on the soft ground near the streams. A baboon ran across my cousin's pathway.

Mr. Nelson came to meet us, for all the villagers had thought that we must be Government officials and had run away. He was a half-caste, and wore a pair of dirty white trousers and a buttonless and filthy pyjama jacket. On his head he had a large brown felt hat, pinned up on one side.

I cannot say that I regarded Mr. Nelson with the

affection that Steve Dunbar had predicted. His eyes were yellow with disease and all vitality had long ago departed from him. In a way he seemed to be nothing at all, nothing but an empty shell, and yet there was something about him, a quality—the lovely woolly phrase sprang to my mind— that defies analysis. His teeth were rotten, and he sucked them constantly with a great deal of noise. And his best friend had quite obviously not told him what he suffered from. He moved slowly and carefully as if he too thought that at any moment the shell might crack.

Strangely enough Mr. Nelson also imagined my cousin to be a Government agent as he entered the village, in spite of his white skin and blond hair, and he immediately asked him what his "privileges" were. Graham must have looked puzzled, for Mr. Nelson asked again how much free rice he was entitled to, and how many labourers he wanted. Graham explained that he had no "privileges," but that he wanted to buy food for his carriers. This seemed to be a problem that puzzled Mr. Nelson a good deal, and one that he was not used to, for, he said, the natives were more used to being *forced* to give than to sell. In that poor starved village they were not used to travellers other than Government officials, who apparently were entitled to take what they wanted, and who passed on their way leaving the villagers even more wretched than they had been before. The rest of their possessions were taken away by Mr. Nelson himself, who, as tax-collector, was entitled to keep a certain percentage of anything he managed to wring out of the natives. As that was far too little to live on, he augmented his income with anything else he could find.

He went to fetch his wife, a black dirty slut, with a small strip of cloth hanging from her waist. Her mouth hung open, and her eyes were vacant, like an idiot's. He brought with him also a dirty piece of old paper on which, in large, childish handwriting, his name was written. It was to prove to us that he really was a civilised man. The effort of walking was almost too much for Mr. Nelson's strength. Fever and sickness had long ago robbed him of all surplus energy. He sank down beside us, almost overcome with the effort, and his wife, having gaped at us, moved away again as slowly and aimlessly as a cow in a field.

After giving Mr. Nelson a few moments to recover himself, Graham tried to encourage him to talk a little about the forthcoming presidential elections. It was a slow process. Sniffing and sucking his teeth between every two or three words, Mr. Nelson proceeded to give us his valuable opinion. Mr. Barclay would certainly be re-elected. Mr. King, who had been President before Mr. Barclay, and who was standing again, had no chance at all. Too many people would lose their jobs. Why, he himself would have to move if Mr. Barclay went out. Mr. King would certainly put one of his own men in his place. Oh, he was very much against Mr. King coming back.

My cousin asked about Mr. Faulkner, who had unsuccessfully contested every election since 1928, who had started the League of Nations inquiry into slavery, and who was spending all of his own money in an endless fight for reform.

"Oh, we don't like Mr. Faulkner," explained Mr. Nelson. "He has an idea."

"What is the idea?" asked my cousin, with interest.

Mr. Nelson breathed hard for a moment, and a little flicker of light burned in his eyes.

"Nobody knows that. But we don't like it."

The light burned out, and for the time being his vitality came to an end. Once again he was only an empty shell. For a few minutes he kept silent, and then with a mighty effort he stood up and slowly managed to drag his diseased body off to his own hut.

The village was certainly wretched, and our hut was dismal. Insects swarmed. When I glanced at the wall of the room where I was to sleep I thought for a moment that it was moving slightly. As I walked closer to examine it I wondered if perhaps I had fever, or if my eyes were playing tricks with me. But it was all right; it was only the insects moving and creeping about.

Now that the natives realised that we were not Government officials and that we were ready to pay for what we had and had no wish to rob them, they crept up to us and sat round our hut. They watched us with interest while we sat writing in our diaries. We were so used to being watched that we no longer noticed it. They became very friendly with our carriers, and in a few moments our headman and the chief were wandering round the village hand-in-hand. Later in the evening they were given good food and palm wine, and we could hear them laughing and dancing during the night, for the fever of the moon was again in their blood.

# CHAPTER X

DEAR Victor Prosser! Of all the people that I met in Liberia, I have retained for him my deepest affections.

He came and sat with us after Mr. Nelson had left, a small, black, earnest little schoolmaster, smiling gently at Graham, for he found out almost immediately that Graham was a Catholic, as he himself was; smiling gently and saying quietly, "That's good. That's very good."

We told him that we would like to take his photograph, and without saying a word he darted away like a little rabbit. He went apparently to change his clothes, for he appeared presently in a pair of shot artificial taffeta trousers in a delicate shade of mauve. Immediately I had taken the photo he held out his hand for the picture, and seemed rather hurt that it was not yet ready for him.

Amadu appeared with some tea for us, and once again Victor Prosser scuttled away. This time he reappeared with an old school copy-book, on the outside of which was written in a child's laboured handwriting, WRITEING AND GOGRAPHY. VICTOR PROSSER. LAWFUL PROPERTY.

"I expect," he said, in his serious, childish way, "that you would like to read this during tea."

"Thank you, we should like to very much," I replied.

"You see," his little black face shone with enthusiasm and the intensity of his feelings, "you see, I read it very day. And I also try to live the way one should. I don't expect *you* will be able to understand that," he explained to me, putting me in one word outside the magic circle of some wider experience. "But," he turned to Graham, "of course *you* understand. And that's good. That's very good." He lingered for a moment. "I hope you will like my writing," he said, and suddenly shy and self-conscious he went away.

He was followed wherever he went by a little primitive native boy with a gun, like a shadow of what he himself had been one day, a perpetual reminder of the great distance that he had travelled—from nothing to the tremendous heights of mauve taffeta trousers.

We opened the book. There was but one page of writing in it, and that was a part of the catechism. We had barely glanced at it when Victor Prosser was again by our side.

"Did you like the writing? I wrote it all by myself."

"It's good," we said kindly, and then we fell into his habit of repeating softly everything we said. "It's very good . . . very good." We asked him about his school, and he said that it was only a few hours' walk from Baplai, in a town called Toweh Ta. As we were all going that way next morning he would walk with us and show us the school. "I trained with the Catholic Fathers in Monrovia," he said proudly. "They said I was good at addition, and quite good at multiplication. Of course," he added, after a little pause, "I did not have time to get as far as fractions."

He looked a little downcast and we changed the subject rapidly.

"Tell us how many pupils you have."

"Forty," he said, his confidence now thoroughly restored. "One of them is my assistant when I am away."

"That must be hard work," we replied, feeling rather sorry for him. "That's difficult . . . very difficult for you."

He smiled. "Oh no. It's easy . . . easy.'

He turned his dreamy eyes to Graham and murmured, "I expect you would like to hear the catechism."

The little schoolmaster was one of those persistently gentle people who, like the very unselfish, invariably get their own way. They fight with weapons that are soft and pliable, and that remain unbroken throughout the longest battles. And who are themselves, in spite of their deceptive, soft appearances, tough and invincible.

Without waiting for an answer, Victor Prosser sent the boy with the gun to fetch an even smaller child, a baby of perhaps three or four, dressed in a little shirt that reached not quite down to his little bulging stomach.

"This is one of my pupils," announced Victor Prosser. "He will read to you."

The child held a book in front of him, but whether it was the right way up or not I could not see. At a tremendous pace he gabbled something off. So far as we were concerned he might have been talking Chinese, for we could not follow one word. But the eyes of Victor Prosser were glowing with a great light. Quite obviously this was his star pupil. Every now and then he interrupted and said, "What is the definition of . . .?" And the child, without drawing breath, would rattle out something in the same old way, without one glimmer of understanding in either his face or voice. But the schoolmaster was delighted, and when the performance was over he turned to me.

"I expect *you* would like to hear some arithmetic," he said, as if I were a creature of some lower order to whom the catechism was something above my power of understanding—as indeed it had been.

"Come along," he said to the child. "Two and two. Hurry up. Hurry up!"

The child looked blank.

"Quick, quick! Two and two! It's four, isn't it?"

"Yes," said the child.

"There!" said the schoolmaster, with the satisfied air of one who has accomplished great things.

Then, quite suddenly, with the unexpectedness of a conjurer, he produced a live chicken, which he presented to us, and murmuring gently he went away.

Mr. Prosser was already waiting for us when we got up next morning. He looked as though he would be a slow walker, so I went on ahead with him, leaving my cousin to pack up the things and catch us up. The forest was thick and dense, and soon Victor Prosser and I were winding our way through the complicated maze of paths. He had his two boys with him, and I had Laminah and one or two of the carriers. There was an early morning silence over everything, and it was still cool. We seemed cut off from the rest of the world by the deep circle of gigantic trees and plants around us—a thick ring, making us a little community separated from the rest of

144

the world. A little band all alone in the early morning hush.

Victor Prosser was in a chatty mood, and was ready, even so early in the morning, to improve the shining hour by acquiring a little more useful knowledge. He had a curious method of asking me questions, for his pride would not allow him to show me that he was uncertain of the answers himself, so he made it appear more as if he were testing *my* knowledge. And when I replied, he would shake his head and whisper, "That's good. That's good."

"London," he said, in a casual off-hand way, "lies on the Tiber, of course, as well as on the Thames."

I did not reply, for I thought that it was just one of his many inaccurate statements of fact, where neither argument, logic, nor reason could convince him of his error. Once an idea had penetrated into the woolly muddle of his mind, nothing could again dislodge it. He would merely shake his head and smile at some deep inner knowledge.

As I did not reply, the question was repeated, and a little impatiently, so I hurriedly answered:

"London is on the Thames, but Rome is on the Tiber."

"Very good. And Queen Elizabeth? Was she Protestant or Catholic?"

"Protestant."

"Mary Queen of Scots?"

"Catholic."

"Just like me."

"Yes, Mr. Prosser, just like you."

He beamed, but the examination went on ruthlessly.

"Sweden and Switzerland are, of course, the same country. Just two names for one thing."

"No," I said firmly. "They are two separate countries."

"Good . . . very good."

We continued for some time and then the path broadened, and he moved beside me and began to whistle.

"Is that God Save the King you are whistling?" I asked, for some of the notes seemed a little out of tune, which made it difficult to recognise. I spoke rather brightly, for, to be honest, I was beginning to get a little tired of answering questions. The forest seemed an incongruous place to choose as an examination-room.

"We will sing God Save the King together. . . ."

I felt a little shy. "Mr. Prosser, I'm afraid my voice is not . . . I mean . . . I don't think, quite honestly, that you will like it very much. You see, it's never been trained. It's not the kind of voice, to be quite honest, that anyone has ever wanted to train."

Mr. Prosser was quite unmoved. I might have been a little piccaninny of three years. "We will now begin."

For some reason, through lack of organisation and co-ordination, we began on different notes, but we smiled and apologised and began again.

A monkey overhead swung itself out of sight. It had my sympathy. Victor Prosser's voice had none of that soft charm that I had expected. It was surprisingly harsh and loud, and extremely untuneful.

"You know Onward Christian Soldiers? Good. We will now sing that. Boys, join in!"

The two little children in front opened wide their mouths and yelled. We all yelled. The forest echoed with our yells. Except for the little piccaninny, we could none of us sing in tune. It was a singularly unpleasant noise.

"That's beautiful," sighed Mr. Prosser. "That's really beautiful. We will sing it again."

He was ready to sing it through a third time, but decided that he was not making the best use of his time, and asked me to tell him about London. In glowing words—of one syllable whenever possible—I described the crowds, the buses, the shops. Into the schoolmaster's eyes there crept a sharp, suspicious look. He was not quite believing me, I felt. I plunged deeper, and described as carefully as I could the underground railways. He had never even seen an ordinary railway, which I had forgotten for the moment, so what I was explaining to him was not only incomprehensible, but sounded extremely untruthful as well.

"Most extraordinary," he said politely, though a little tartly.

"But I think we will now sing the Liberian National Anthem. Boys, join in!"

He was right, of course. It was an impossible, crazy world that I had described. I laughed to myself to think that I had been such a fool as to imagine that I would find dangers in Liberia. Here it was safe and quiet. I looked round me and found nothing but peace. But the London I had described of crowds, and hurrying motor vehicles, noise and underground trains, that was terrifying. It all sounded horrible, and I almost felt that I did not want to go back—till, of course, I remembered Elizabeth Arden, my flat, and the Savoy Grill.

I did not know the verses of the Liberian National Anthem, but joined lustily in the chorus:

"In joy and gladness with our hearts united,
    We'll shout the freedom of a land benighted.
    Long live Liberia, happy land,
    A home of glorious liberty by God's command."

Behind me I heard a new but equally unmelodious voice. I turned round and saw Graham's grinning, delighted face. And so through the heart of the African jungle we wound our singing ways. As we approached Toweh Ta, Victor Prosser became excited. We stopped singing while he told us about his school. It was difficult to keep the boys, he said, for they so often ran away to their homes, but he had one or two excellent pupils. They would all be busy now at their work, he announced, pulling out a big watch. Half-past nine. He would take us to see them, and tell one of them to recite the catechism to Graham. He painted us a glowing picture of the exhibition of industry that we would see going on. His young assistant would be taking the class. They would all be hard at work.

Trembling with excitement he took us into the compound and led us up to the class-room. As headmaster he underwent a subtle change, and after putting on a pair of spectacles he opened the door with a flourish and waved us in first. He followed. Then we all looked at one another in horror. The room was empty. There was no class going on, and nowhere was there a sign of a boy.

We all three felt flat and rather silly, as if we had arrived at a party on the wrong day.

The young assistant came ambling in, and Victor Prosser, with wrath in his voice, demanded the reason why there was no class. The young man in great agitation replied that by his watch it was only eight-forty-five. We all looked at our watches and they were each one completely different. For some reason we all put them to nine o'clock, and the assistant rang the bell for school. But the spell was broken, and poor Victor Prosser felt that he could no longer impress us with his efficiency. We praised the buildings, the cleanliness, and every thing else that we could think of. Then, as a parting gift to our friend, we produced an old Geographical Magazine that we had taken by mistake from Ganta, and presented it to him. His sad little face lit up, and he opened it and looked at the pictures. But we could see what he really wanted.

"Won't you read us a little?" we asked.

With a beaming smile Victor Prosser read out a few sentences, leaving out completely, as if they did not exist, all the difficult words. It made no sense, but it warmed our hearts to see him happy once more.

"That's good," we said. "That's very good."

"Yes," said Victor Prosser, "that's very good."

And he turned and walked proudly into the classroom.

The walk after we left Victor Prosser was appallingly dull, and I could think of nothing to think about. I tried to think of games to play—timing the number of minutes it would take to walk a thousand steps, or counting the monkeys. I wondered how Graham was feeling, for his face had been grey again that morning and the nerve twitching slightly. I did not dare say anything or offer any sympathy, and he never complained. We were both a little frightened, I think, by the power of suggestion, and felt it was better to leave it alone and to see what his strong will power and determination could do.

It was very hot. My thick shoes were beginning to wear out and I could feel the sharp stones pierce into my feet through the soles. My shirt was full of holes, caused by the rats and cockroaches. Laminah, walking just behind me, was unable for once to contribute anything towards a general feeling of gaiety, for he was moaning and holding his cheek in his hand. I turned round and promised him "plenty good medicine" that evening. Our cook was an old man, and he was beginning to find the walking difficult. He never complained, but we often had to wait for him to catch us up. In one hand he carried an open knife, and in the other a live chicken. His long robes had got so torn that he often stumbled over the trailing ends. He held us back, so that although we were not walking on hilly ground, our progress was slow. The hours dragged by, and I longed for a good wide view. At last we stumbled into Greh. The chief's young son could speak English.

"I am Samuel Johnson," he announced.

I felt as if we had strayed into a lunatic asylum, and felt a strong desire to answer, "I am Queen Elizabeth."

The village was extremely primitive, and Graham and I crawled into several huts to try and find one we could sleep in. They were dirty and built so low that it was

150

impossible to stand straight in them. At last my cousin announced that he would sleep in the open palaver house in the middle of the village, and told the boys to put up our beds there. Amadu was horrified, his conventional nature was shaken to its foundations. The house had no walls and we would be completely exposed to the gaze of the entire village all night. We were firm and Amadu sadly obeyed.

The chief's son had been educated on the coast, and had brought back some strange things into this most primitive village. A naked boy was wandering round with an open umbrella, and there were some odd pictures of "civilised life" in our sleeping quarters. Two sexual perverts were wandering naked round the village with their arms round each others necks. For hours they would stand and gaze at Graham, which he found extremely trying. It was the only time that we saw such a thing among the natives, and we could only think that that too had come up from the coast. The whole place was an unpleasant mixture of the extremely primitive and the worst bits of a seedy civilisation.

We were all beginning to feel over-tired. This was not only caused by the long treks through the forest, but also through lack of sleep. We were always up by five o'clock in the morning, but as it was the evening in the villages that made the whole trip worth while, we were never in bed as early as we should have been. Also our food was getting appallingly monotonous—hot, stringy chicken and rice for supper, and cold, stringy chicken for lunch, day after day. The cook luckily knew of a great many different methods of preparing eggs, but somehow an egg's an egg for all that. Sometimes he also did things with the big wild bananas that we could occasionally get hold of. They were not good to eat raw, but it was possible, though they were heavy and indigestible, to swallow them after they had been cooked. They provided a change, anyway.

We had carefully divided up our last few biscuits between us. I ate mine quickly, for I have never yet mastered the art of saving for a rainy day, but Graham had more self-control and managed to spin his out for a day or two. We were also finishing our last tin of precious Golden Syrup, which meant the last of our sweet things, except for a very little sugar. We had opened our last tin of butter, and it had gone bad. The whisky was running short. There was no fruit, and the cigarettes were coming to an end, which was rather an agony in that land of flies.

The quickly emptying food boxes were a depressing sight when we examined them, but it actually seems worse looking back on it all than it did at the time. It was then more of a bore than anything, and I suppose it was because there was simply nothing that we could do about it, and so we did not worry very seriously. We were glad that we had bought another large tin of Epsom salts from Dr. Harley in Ganta, for all our men were now clamouring for it and we got through an enormous amount each day. The carriers had got hold of some cow for their supper, and in chopping it up with a sword our second headman had chopped off the top of his finger. Graham and I had just finished dealing out the various medicines, treating nasty sores and calming

Laminah by giving him bogus medicine for his tooth, and we were now quite ready for a well-deserved rest. We were horribly, horribly tired, and it was almost more than we could bear when the carrier came rushing towards us with blood flowing from him in great spurts. Patiently we had to put on iodine while he screamed and yelled with pain. I tore up a not very clean handkerchief to make a bandage, and we bound him up while he howled and the blood poured over us and all our things. His screams left me callously indifferent. It was too hot and we were far too tired to waste energy in pity.

We ate our supper and wondered why we never quarrelled. Every one had told us that we would, but we never did. Perhaps it was because we seemed to have an instinctive feeling about what would annoy or irritate the other, and so we managed to keep off dangerous topics.

Graham lit a cigarette and the villagers screamed with fright. All round us the carriers were sitting in little groups. They were too tired to dance, and even the cow for supper had been unable to rouse their spirits.

I went to bed, first kicking out all the goats and dogs in the hut. But they soon came back, for there was nothing that could keep them out, and just before I fell into a heavy, exhausted sleep I heard them sniffing at our things, and knocking over our cases.

It was just getting light as I woke up next morning. Amadu was standing by Graham's bed explaining that Laminah was too bad to go on that day. "Poor Graham," I thought. "He has all the work to do." And I shut my eyes and fell asleep again.

It was perfectly true. When I woke up again it was daylight, and my cousin was dressed and had arranged everything. As far as one could tell there was nothing wrong with Laminah's tooth, but he was suffering badly from shock. We did not want to stay in Greh, and my cousin suggested that Laminah should remain behind with one of the men for another day, while we went on to Tappee Ta and waited for him there. Tappee Ta was a big town we had heard, with a District Commissioner, and we would be far more comfortable. Laminah refused point-blank to be left. We were still in cannibal country, and he would rather die on the way with us than be left without our protection. So we put him in my hammock and he lay rolled up in a little black ball, with his woolly cap pulled right over his ears, moaning softly. He looked a little as if he might die, not because he was very ill, but because he seemed suddenly to have thrown aside all fighting spirit, as if he no longer wanted to make any effort to live. He did this so thoroughly that though Amadu tried to rouse him, he lay quite still in the hammock ready to deliver up his spirit. Luckily this state of affairs did not last long, for when he discovered that Tappee Ta was a big place, with all kinds of exciting things going on, he pulled himself together in one minute and recovered.

After a few hours walk we came suddenly to a wide road, with men cutting down trees on either side. It meant a hot walk and, of course, it was as rough as the jungle tracks, but I was enormously impressed. Here was one of the roads that the President had told us about, and his words floated back to my mind. "I can make roads as good as those in America or England. We will soon have motor-cars. We will have aeroplanes. . . ." The men were cutting down gigantic trees. There was always a little orchestra of drums and rattles playing beside them to keep them in rhythm. It was the first sign I had seen of the President's roads. I did not know then that though the President might have ideas as far-seeing as Hitler's, he had none of the famous Prussian organisation behind him to help him carry out his ideas. So many roads did we see abandoned unfinished, and never one did we see that was suitable for motor traffic.

The sun beat down on our heads. I had been used to wearing no hat in the forest, and now found it troublesome to put on a thick double felt. I took it off again, trusting that my thick mop of hair would prevent my getting sunstroke, but I was glad when the President's road came to an abrupt end, and we were once more out of the glare. The carriers no longer sang or danced as they walked. We all needed every bit of energy and, apart from Laminah's moans, we were a long, silent snake that wound its tortuous way through the forest.

Luck, as usual, was with us. As we got near to Tappee Ta we heard that Col. Davis was there. Col. Davis, known as the Dictator of Grand Bassa, the head of the Liberian Army, the man responsible for all the atrocities described in the British Blue Book, who had led the infamous campaign against the Chief Nimley, murdering callously (the blue book said) unprotected women and children. A cold-blooded man, I thought, a soldier of Fortune. He had served in a black regiment in Mexico, and seen service in the Philippines, had drifted somehow over to Liberia, and had quickly worked himself up to an important position in Liberian politics. He was a man of importance now, and I was interested to meet him.

# CHAPTER XI

AS soon as we arrived in Tappee Ta the men with one accord either threw themselves flat in the dust outside the District Commissioner's compound, or they put down their heavy burdens and sat on them with their heads hanging down on their knees. Mark led me to one of the food boxes and told me to sit down and rest till Graham had finished arranging where we were to stay. We were all exhausted, and Laminah was still moaning. The heavy damp heat seemed to have soaked right into our bodies, making us feel as if our bones were rotting. I felt that if a fire should break out around us we would stay exactly where we were—too tired to bother to save ourselves. My cousin had gone inside the compound, for as usual he had all the work to do. There was no rest for him till every little detail had been attended to, everything arranged for all those under his care.

Someone—I cannot remember who it was—came up to me and asked me to come into the compound. He was a chatty young man, and kept up a flow of conversation. A bugle was blowing as we entered, and a stream of people was moving towards an open hut, and settling themselves inside, packing closely together one against another. After they had somehow managed to squeeze in, a smart, upright figure in a white uniform walked briskly across the compound to the hut.

"Colonel Davis," said my companion, waving a hand at the soldierly figure, and then went on to explain to me that all the chiefs of the district had sent complaints to Monrovia against their Commissioners, that the Government had at last decided to take action and had sent up Col. Davis to arrange a kind of trial to settle the whole matter. The chiefs and the District Commissioners were now all gathered together, and the trial was taking some days. Mr. Wordsworth, the Commissioner of Tappee Ta was very much hated, and was apparently considered one of the worst offenders.

Graham was waiting for me in one of the little houses round the compound.

"This is your house," said the small black man at my side, bowing slightly as if he were formally introducing me to it, and then, pointing to a small drab building next to it, he added in a tired, but, nevertheless, peculiarly sinister voice. "And that is the prison." He paused a moment while I glanced across to it. "And now," he said sharply, "I would like to see your papers."

I jumped at the unexpectedness of the request, for it was the first time since we had got to Liberia that we had been asked for them. I blushed and felt that I looked guilty, for I knew quite well that our papers were not in order. We had permits only for the Western provinces of Liberia and for the coast, but had no right to be where we were. I hurriedly put on my vaguest manner, and behaving as if I had not quite understood, I ambled away, looking as absent-minded as I could, and left Graham to deal with the situation.

I walked towards the prison, and studied it from every side. It was not pleasant. It was a small, dark hut, and out of the little windows gaunt and hungry faces were gaping. Men and women, tied by ropes to the bars across the windows, were staring out into the compound. Inside I could imagine it would be suffocatingly hot, a second black hole of Calcutta. A few of the prisoners were lying outside, tied by the leg to wooden posts, in the glowing heat, unable to get into the shade. They all wore the heavy, stupid expressions of animals, and when the warders beat them with clubs, they seemed hardly to feel the blows.

I was glad when I returned to our house to find that Graham had somehow managed to get over all difficulties about our papers, for I had no wish to experience life in the Tappee Ta prison.

I had a rest on my bed and woke up feeling better. Graham looked very unwell. He was longing to get down to the coast, but had decided that we should stay at Tappee Ta for two or three days to give the men a rest. I was glad, for I was still enjoying myself, and I had a very strong instinct that I was going to dislike the life on the coast. Although I was very worried about Graham, I liked to linger inland as long as possible. My cousin had certainly caught some strange internal disease. He felt sick, and yet he was hungry all the time, and I wondered what was the right treatment for him. We had so little medicine with us, and were forced to put our entire trust in Epsom salts.

159

The palaver was over by five, and the stream of people oozed out of the hut once more. Col. Davis marched smartly, but with all the attractive swagger and confidence of a successful adventurer, across to his own house. I liked the swagger, the proud, slightly insolent tilt of the head, the clean well-fitting uniform, and the clear rather too-loud voice ringing across the compound. No longer could I think of him as a cold-blooded murderer of women and children. His personality was too colourful, his gestures were too theatrical. He looked the part of the handsome villain in an old-fashioned melodrama, who, in the last moments of the third act repents, and with extravagant expressions of emotion proves that underneath his dashing exterior there lies a heart of gold.

Mr. Wordsworth came to see if we had everything we wanted. He was a half-caste with yellow eyes, black side-whiskers, and an expression of appalling ferocity. To our surprise his manner when he spoke was painfully shy and timid, and it was hard to think of him as having oppressed the natives. He was nervous, and glanced from time to time across the compound to the house where Col. Davis was staying. It was difficult to understand the reason why he was scared, for Col. Davis was his cousin, and family relationships mean a great deal in Liberia; and it looked as though the trial had been arranged simply to calm the chiefs. We were quite certain that Mr. Wordsworth would not be removed from Tappee Ta.

The Commissioner was followed everywhere by his younger brother, who introduced himself as the Quartermaster. He was a small seedy individual with an over-friendly manner, who buzzed round us with the tire-some insistence of a mosquito. It was impossible to shake him off. "I like you both very much," he said from time to time, as if he expected us to be pleased about it.

Graham sent a note over to Col. Davis asking for an interview, and presently a message came back to say that although Col. Davis was very tired after a hard day's work, he would see my cousin for just a few moments.

I sat on the verandah and waited. After an hour it got dark and there was still no sign of Graham. I called for a lamp, and got out the stories of Saki and Somerset Maugham, and tried to read. At last, a long while after our usual supper time, I saw two figures crossing the compound towards me. They were talking earnestly together like old friends.

I was introduced to Col. Davis, and we shook hands.

"We want some whisky," said Graham.

"I usually drink Ovaltine," the Dictator of Grand Bassa explained to me. "But just to-night——"

"Of course," I murmured.

He was a good-looking man, tall and straight, with a neat black-pointed beard. Unfortunately he had too many gold teeth, so that his flashing smile lost a good deal of its charm. He made use of his hands in dramatic gestures as he spoke, and his black face and eyes were full of expression. At the moment he was playing the part of the man of the world, and once again I felt my shorts were too short. He described his tour through Europe a few years before with Mr. King, the President at that time, but managed to give the impression that none of the entertainments that had been arranged for them could compare with the elegance and taste of the dinner-parties of Monrovia.

"I understand you can no longer obtain the Russian cigarette in London," he murmured, helping himself liberally to the whisky. "Of course in Monrovia we can still manage to get them. At our parties they form a course in themselves."

"At the end?" asked my cousin.

"Oh no. After the fish and before the salad the lights are lowered and each guest quietly smokes one cigarette."

My cousin gently brought the conversation back to Liberian politics, and Col. Davis seemed ready to talk with animation on any subject that we chose. That he was a clever man there could be no doubt, for no other man had managed to remain in office under Mr. Barclay after Mr. King had been forced to resign, following the League of Nations' inquiry into Liberian affairs. Mr. King had collapsed completely during the investigations into the shipping of forced labour to Fernando Po, and although he was now standing again in the presidential elections, at that time he had got out quickly enough and without putting forward any defence whatever. But Col. Davis had stayed on and become right man to Mr. Barclay. He was clever, he was efficient, and he was brave. When Graham mentioned the Kru war and the official report of his part in it, tears nearly came into his eyes. He had been sent down to collect taxes that had never been paid, from the district of Chief Nimley. The chief opposed him, and apparently the troops had got out of hand.  The report of the British Consul showed that Col. Davis had displayed amazing personal courage, but a ghastly picture had been drawn of wholesale murder and destruction.

"They say I murdered children, little helpless children. I, who love babies.  I couldn't do it.  Do you know that I am the head of the Boy Scouts of Liberia?  Do you know that every night I read stories to my children before they go to sleep?  Ask my wife.  She would tell you that I do."

"I'm sure you do," we both said.

"My wife is a charming woman," he added, in less tragic tones.  "You would like her very much.  She is my second wife.  My first wife was a teetotaller when I first married her.  She was nice, too, but I had to cure her.  It wasn't easy, but I guess I managed to do it.  But my second wife is very charming.  She would tell you how I love little children.  And my mother in America . . . she wrote to tell me that she did not believe those stories.  And she ought to know me.  She loves me very much.  She is a charming woman too."

Col. Davis' boy interrupted for a moment to tell him that his supper had been ready for a long time, but he was waved away impatiently, and the Colonel helped himself to a little more whisky.

"Liberia is a beautiful country," he continued.  Words poured out of his mouth, as if a hidden tap had been turned on.  "A beautiful country.  I ought to know.  I guess I've seen most of the world.  But when I hear the young men in Monrovia saying they want to see Europe or America, I say to them—see Liberia first.  And I think that's a beautiful thought. See Liberia first. That's what I say—see Liberia first."

He had a great deal of charm, the indefinable, reckless charm of the man who follows no laws except his own, and who has lived all his life on his wits. He told us of his adventures, and his many hairbreadth escapes, though he never quite explained how it was that he landed up in Liberia. But he told us that soon after he arrived he was made medical officer of health, although, I believe, he possessed no medical degree. Later he became the chief of the Frontier Forces, and with bravery and an attractive coolheadedness had quickly organised the disarming of the natives. It was an amazing achievement and Col. Davis was rightly proud of it. Now he was one of the most powerful men in Liberia.

At last he had to go. It was getting late, and he had a heavy day's work ahead of him in the stuffy little palaver-house. Though he had probably settled the verdict in his mind before the trial had even begun, he managed very cleverly to soothe the chiefs, by listening to their complaints patiently to the end. He had also decided that if he had time he would try some of the prisoners in the dingy prison next to our house.

"There's a wretched woman there who makes a lot of trouble throwing lightning at the people she does not like. A member of the Buzie tribe, of course. We must stamp that out. We can't have that sort of thing going on. I guess I'll have to give her a hard sentence."

He was ready to go on talking again, but his boy appeared once more just as his hand was straying towards the bottle. He remembered that it was late and so, with a last flash of his gold teeth, he marched briskly out into the night.

The night for some reason was bitterly cold, and I tossed and turned on my hard bed, shivering as though I had fever. At last I could stand it no more, and slipping my mackintosh over my pyjamas I went out for a little walk. It was very quiet as I left the compound, and I felt a little frightened. My footsteps seemed to echo noisily in the stillness. It was the hour before dawn, and the grey light lay thickly over everything, so that the huts and trees looked colourless and strange. I walked down to the edge of the forest and stood behind one of the leopard traps. Nothing moved. No wild beast came slinking towards me. Everything lay in a deep and heavy sleep. The little pathway leading into the thick, dead forest seemed as mysterious as life itself. For a few yards one could see the way clearly enough, and then it turned a little corner and disappeared into the unknown. Slowly I walked back to the village. No one moved. No one heard me pass by. I felt as lonely as a ghost must feel, and I longed to wake up Graham and ask him to walk with me. But he needed sleep, and so I lingered by myself for a little while longer among the round mud huts, and as dawn was breaking I went home and back again to my bed.

DEAR FRIEND MR. GREENE,

Good morning. I'm about to ask a favour of you this morning, which I hope you will be able to grant. If you have any Brandy, kindly send me a little, or anything else if Brandy is out. Same would be very appreciated by me. I'm feeling very, very cold this a.m. you know. I hope you both well.

"With best wishes for your health,

"Your friend,

WORDSWORTH, *Quartermaster*.

P.S.—I'll bring my sisters to pay a visit to you and cousin this p.m. as they would like her for their friend.

It was very early in the morning when we received this friendly little note, and for the rest of the day young Mr. Wordsworth hovered round us. He was hungry for friendship and admiration, and wasted his energy performing little tasks for us that he imagined would give us pleasure, and that only succeeded in irritating us. "We will write to each other," he said from time to time. "We will tell each other everything. We are friends, and I like you very much."

He described to us the delights of Monrovia, till I began to wonder whether my instinct about the capital of Liberia was perhaps a little unfair. It looked as if I might get a pleasant shock if we ever really managed to arrive there. From all accounts it appeared to be a miniature Paris set down incongruously on the West coast of Africa.

"Monrovia in the season. There are lights, there are cafés. Music, dinners, and dancing on the beach by moonlight. Excitements all the time. Pleasures of every description. Of course you will be a little late. You will miss the height of the gaiety, but at any time it is always a wonderful city."

And then he painted a picture of himself as the popular bachelor about town, run after by the girls, admired and envied by the men. Poor, pathetic little man. It was all a description of life as he would like it to have been, and it existed only in his second-rate little mind. His thoughts were highly coloured by things and places he had read about in cheap novelettes, in tales of gilded life, of champagne and amorous adventures. The tumbled-down houses of Monrovia became palaces when seen through his eyes, the empty rough roads were smooth streets along which big, purring cars slipped swiftly past. The little tin sheds where one could buy cheap cane juice became exciting halls of pleasure. And he himself was no longer an ugly, unhealthy little man, but handsome and gay, and the centre of attraction, like the pictures he had seen of sleek youths in the American advertisements of How to Develop your Charm. His eyes glowed as he described these delights to us. They were quite real to him. His imagination laid fingers of gold on everything, and turned the very dust in the air to diamonds.

And so we listened to his stories, and every now and then his elder brother, the District Commissioner, would come and join our little group. He would stand glowering fiercely at us, and if we made any attempt to draw him into the conversation he would become embarrassed and move away awkwardly.

Col. Davis joined us again during the evening, and as I poured out his whisky I apologised to him that we had no Ovaltine to offer him. He forgave us readily and did not seem to mind, and quickly changed the subject by promising to send for some snake dancers to perform for us—strange little girls who could twist their bodies around like the boneless wonders at a circus—or a cabaret dancer on the rising floor at midnight. And yet they remained—apparently—as graceful and delicate as a Chinese poem. He also presented us with a guide who would lead us down to the coast, a horrid little boy called Tommy, who wore an ugly blue uniform and had an appallingly aggressive manner. We disliked him from the first, and as time went on so did our dislike grow into a raging hatred. He was a peculiarly unpleasant child, with all the worst faults and not one of the graces of youth.

Graham was very unwell.

"That's strange," said Col. Davis. "I guess I know the world, and Liberia is the healthiest country I've ever been in. Never had a day's illness since I landed."

"What about fever?"

"Fever? Never seen a mosquito since the day I arrived. Excellent climate. I guess if the rest of the world knew about it they would rush up to our hills for a health holiday. That's one of the reasons why I say to our youngsters—see Liberia first."

Sipping his whisky, he grew sentimental. "I've been glad to see you," he said simply. "Do you know what the captain of a ship once told me way out in mid-ocean? He pointed to the little lights of a boat passing by and—'Davis,' he said, 'I have three books in my library. The first one is called *Ships that Pass in the Night*.'" Col. Davis looked at us softly. "Can you guess what the others were?" he asked.

"No," said Graham.

"*The People we Meet* was the second, and then the captain looked at me for a long time and finally he said, 'The third book is called *The People we Love.*' I guess that's a beautiful thought."

We all finished our drinks and sat in silence thinking it out.

At last the Colonel shook us by the hand warmly. "I must go," he said. "But we will meet to-morrow."

Alas! We did not see Col. Davis again. Next day he was unable to get up. He lay in bed with a raging fever.

Our men had recovered their spirits and Laminah had already forgotten that he had ever had toothache, and so the time seemed ripe for us to leave Tappee Ta.

Young Mr. Wordsworth stayed close to us, revelling in our companionship to the last moment, promising to write us endless letters, and envying us our days in Monrovia. "But all the same," he added philosophically, "they have some extraordinarily good things up here. I've just heard of a wonderful cure for venereal disease. I expect you would like to know what it is, although it is a secret of the Buzie tribe. I haven't tried it myself yet, but I hear it's very good. It's quite simple. You just tie a rope round your middle. That's all you do, but they tell me it works well. It's worth trying. I thought you would like to know about it."

And he said good night, happy in the belief that he had told us something that was worth knowing.

# CHAPTER XII

AS we collected our things together in the early morning ready to trek down to Zigi's town, I wished suddenly that we could stay on in Tappee Ta. Graham looked ghastly, and was shivering. He had a strange, stupid expression on his face, and sometimes he stumbled slightly as though he could not see very well. I was frightened, for I realised that he was seriously ill. It was no good asking him to stay in Tappee Ta till he was better. He had made up his mind that he must get to the coast as quickly as possible. Although he knew that Grand Bassa was a small town and possessed only one white inhabitant, he talked incessantly about it, as if it was going to turn out to be a heaven on earth. I did not argue with him, for I could see that he was determined to press on. He was as obstinate as only a sick man can be. He wanted to get to the coast, and he wanted to get there quickly.

To be alone with one companion for several weeks on end in uncomfortable and strange surroundings means that one either becomes very fond of him or grows to dislike him intensely. There is no half-way house. Mere indifference is impossible. Luckily during these last few weeks I had discovered that I liked Graham, and I had learnt to look up to him and respect him.

As I saw him in the early morning light, his face grey and drawn, his hand shaking even more than it usually did as he poured the Epsom salts into his tea, I became scared. I could not bear to see him so ill, and to be altogether unable to help. I felt stupid and useless.

Young Mr. Wordsworth had got up early to wish us good-bye, and tried to detain us with chatty bits of gossip. As the snake dancers had never turned up, he promised us that he would send a message to tell them to go straight to Zigi's town and to perform to us that evening. Col. Davis, he added, was still very ill and would not be getting up for several days. He began to tell us, almost with tears in his eyes, that we were now his best friends. We were not modest enough to feel flattered by these sentiments, and merely felt slightly embarrassed, for we wanted to be off as quickly as possible. At last we had to tell him that we, too, liked him very much, and that all through our lives we would remember to write him long letters telling him of our adventures in the gay world, and that his friendship would warm our hearts for ever. As we were talking we had begun to edge away, till at last the distance between us became so great that we were no longer able to catch his emotional words of eternal love; but we waved to him as kindly as it is possible to wave, and went on. He stood, a pathetic little figure, by the gateway of the compound, and watched us till we disappeared into the forest.

Even on that day, in spite of his pains, Graham was walking on ahead. I could see his stockings slipping down to his ankles, but young Mr. Wordsworth had filled the air with such an emotional atmosphere that instead of being irritated I became morbid.

"Perhaps," I thought, "I shall never see them slip down again."

Tommy, the young boy given to us by Col. Davis to guide us to the coast, started off by walking at a brisk pace ahead of us all. He carried an old gun over his shoulder. It was so old and broken that it was obviously useless, and in his right hand he carried an old tin pail, at the bottom of which lay his few possessions. After half an hour he was tired of walking on ahead and began to take long rests in every village that we passed through. Aggressively he demanded palm wine and food from the villagers and they gave him everything he wanted, for he wore a uniform, and that scared them so that they dared not ask for payment. As a servant of Col. Davis he considered himself a Government official and therefore entitled to help himself to whatever he wanted. He stole right and left, and put his winnings into the tin pail. As a guide he was inefficient, for he was soon lagging far behind our caravan, stopping at the villages and bullying every one he could. We had just finished our lunch and were ready to go on when Tommy caught us up and asked us to linger a little longer while he had a little sleep. There was a blissful, dreamy smile on his face, and he was more than a little drunk. He sat down, laughing and smiling, and hugging the tin pail that was full of stolen property. He was in that happy state that is strongly fortified against any reproofs, and we walked away and left him to follow on. As a guide, we felt, Tommy was not going to be a great success.

Although he was feeling so ill, Graham ate an enormous lunch. His eternal hunger seemed to be one of the symptoms of his strange illness. After lunch he raced on ahead again, refusing to walk more slowly, and looking every moment as if he were going to faint. We were still walking downhill. The air was as damp as the hottest of the greenhouses at Kew Gardens. There was thunder in the air again. We could hear it rumbling in the distance. We had no idea how far we were from the coast. Some said ten days, others said a week, but no one seemed to know.

"Only two days," lied Mark brightly, thinking it would cheer me up.

"Two more weeks," lied Laminah, knowing that I liked the villages and thinking that that was what I would like to hear.

I gave it up.

We had nine hours steady walking to Zigi's town. The forest now seemed more luxuriant; it was greener and looked less dead. I thought I might find some orchids, but it seemed to be the wrong season for them, and I saw only little pink star-like flowers.

"De cook plenty tired," said Laminah to me. There was nothing I could do for the old man. We were all plenty tired. Our carriers no longer joked or sang. We walked silently and no one spoke. The atmosphere grew heavier and the thunder got louder.

Graham was tottering as we got to Zigi's town; he was staggering as though he was a little drunk. He could get no rest from the carriers while he was up, for they came to him as usual with all their troubles, but I managed to persuade him to go to bed. I took his temperature and it was very high. I gave him plenty of whisky and Epsom salts, and covered him with blankets, hoping that I was doing the right thing.

I had supper by myself while the thunder roared; and the boys served me with grave faces. The same thought was in all our minds. Graham would die. I never doubted it for a minute. He looked like a dead man already. The stormy atmosphere made my head ache and the men quarrelsome. I could hear them snapping at each other, but I left them alone.

I took Graham's temperature again, and it had gone up. I felt quite calm at the thought of Graham's death. To my own horror I felt unemotional about it. My mind kept telling me that I was really very upset, but actually I was so tired that though I could concentrate easily on the practical side of it all, I was incapable of feeling anything. I worked out quietly how I would have my cousin buried, how I would go down to the coast, to whom I would send telegrams. I had no fear of going on alone, for I realised by this time that with the help of Amadu I would be perfectly safe. Only one thing worried me in the most extraordinary way. Graham was a Catholic, and into my muddled, weary brain came the thought that I ought to burn candles for him if he died. I was horribly upset, for we had no candles. I could not remember why I should burn candles, but I felt vaguely that his soul would find no peace if I could not do that for him. All night I was troubled by this thought. It seemed to me desperately important.

To cheer myself up I smoked an extra cigarette after

supper. We had only a few left, but the insects were bad and I was getting covered with bugs again. Laminah came to me from time to time to tell me that the snake dancers were on their way. I did not believe him—rightly as it turned out—but I appreciated the instinct that made him ready to tell me anything, however untrue, that might please me. Later when I went to bed I found that he had taken considerable trouble in decorating my bed with posies of little pink flowers. He had done it charmingly and grinned with delight when I told him that it had given me pleasure.

I tried to write up my diary. It needed a good deal of will-power now to concentrate on it every day. The temptation to put it off till another time was very great, but I knew that if I once gave in I should find it very difficult to start again. To my surprise I find now that although I mentioned casually that I was a little tired, I added: "Feeling very fit indeed. This weather agrees with me, but the carriers all have bad headaches." Looking back it seems to me that I was extremely tired that evening, but I suppose that I was getting used to the feeling and that it was only when I got to the coast that I realised that I was not quite as fresh as I had imagined.

It was a pleasant little village. I walked through it, enjoying, as I always did, the friendliness of the natives. Laminah and Mark came with me, but I told them I was not in the mood to talk, and with graceful understanding they immediately dropped ten yards behind me, giving me the feeling that I was alone and yet showing me that they were there to protect me. Amadu stayed within hearing distance of Graham. They were doing their best to try to make me understand that whatever happened, they would never forget that they had given their word in Freetown that they would protect us to the end of the journey. It was only that evening in Zigi's town that I realised how much I cared for our boys, and what valuable and loyal friends they were.

Tommy, on the other hand, was drunk again and rolling tipsyly and noisily round the village. He seemed to be under the impression that I liked him, and he wanted to walk hand in hand with me, till the boys through their superior physical strength had proved to him that he was mistaken.

The storm broke and I hurried back to my hut as the rains came down. It was a big hut with two rooms, and before I went to bed I went and had another look at Graham. He was in a restless doze, muttering to himself, and soaked in perspiration.

I went to my room, but did not dare to sleep very much in case my cousin should call out. Outside the rains descended, but I had a well-built hut this time and none of the water splashed through the roof. I felt rather cosy as I lay snugly in bed while the thunder roared outside.

To my great surprise Graham was not dead in the morning. I was quite amazed, and gazed at him for some moments without speaking. I went into his room expecting to see him either delirious or gasping out his last few breaths, and I found him up and dressed. He looked terrible. A kind of horrid death's head grinned at me. His cheeks had sunk in, there were thick black smudges under his eyes, and his scrubby beard added nothing of beauty to the general rather seedy effect. His expression, however, was more normal, for the uncanny harsh light that had glowed in his eyes the day before, had disappeared. I took his temperature and it was very subnormal.

"We must go on quickly," he said. "I'm all right again."

"Won't you rest just one day?" I asked.

"No," said Graham impatiently. "We must get down to the coast."

The coast. My cousin was craving to get down to the coast as a pilgrim might crave to get to a holy city.

I went out and got hold of the boys and told them to find out how far it was to Grand Bassa. Tommy, I thought, might know, or perhaps the chief.

"Two days," said Mark.

"Two weeks," said Laminah.

"Oh, my God," I said.

I asked the headman, "How far Grand Bassa? Ask chief."

He gave his lovely vague smile, and said softly, "Too far." And all round me like an angry chorus the carriers echoed, "Too far, too far."

Graham hired two extra men so that he could use a hammock occasionally, and we set off. But the hammock made him feel sick, and he did not use it much. As we were walking, Laminah gave me a sudden push to the side. I wondered what he was doing, and then realised that I had almost stepped on to a large black snake, and I stood still a moment and watched it glide away into the undergrowth.

I had put bits of cardboard into my shoes so that I would not feel the sharp stones pressing through my thin soles. But it was very uncomfortable and I had to take them out again. Luckily it was only a short trek of three hours—our last short walk—but by the time we got to our destination Graham's temperature was up again.

Apart from a few women and children, Bassa town was empty when we arrived. The men had killed an elephant, and they were now away cutting it up and dividing the meat among themselves. Elephant meat is considered a great delicacy among the natives, but having once smelt it at a native market, I had no wish ever to eat it. But I was sorry not to see the elephant, for we had come across none of the "hundreds of elephants" that Steve Dunbar at Sacrepie had prophesied that we would see, and, to be honest, I had not really believed in their existence. However, this elephant was some distance away, and the men were not expected back till morning.

I wondered how the carriers would behave themselves in that village of women. So far on the trip they seem to have kept to the straight and narrow path, but I had my misgivings as to what that night might bring forth. However, next morning there were no complaints, so apparently, whatever had happened, all was well.

As a matter of fact there was one man in the village, a kind of very minor District Commissioner, who told us, somewhat vaguely, that he had been sent up to improve the place. He did not tell us how he meant to achieve that worthy object. It would have been interesting to know, for he looked stupid, lazy, and unimaginative. We asked him how far it was to Grand Bassa, and he stood and thought for a very long while, moving his lips as though he were working out an intricate mathematical problem.

"Seven days," he said, at last. We thought he must know as he had only just come up that way.

Rice for the men was expensive, so we realised that we must be getting nearer civilisation. For the sake of something to do, I watched the men cook their supper, and noticed with amusement that they used our bath as their saucepan. It was a miserable-looking meal they had, with none of that rich, yellow, evil-smelling sauce that they liked so much. Just rice and a few scraggy bones of some unidentifiable animal.

There was another sign that we were getting nearer the "civilisation" that I was dreading so much. A young girl, an obvious little prostitute, hovered round and postured in front of Graham. She was a beautiful little creature, and I felt sure that at some time she had been down to the coast and that she had known white men. She was cute and intelligent, but over-optimistic, or she would have realised at once that my cousin was beyond noticing anything. It was strange to find her in that village, and I wondered why she had come back to her primitive home. Again I had a sudden fear that "civilisation" was about to destroy some of the charm and beauty of the village life. It had hardly touched it there as yet; just the tip of its finger had left one or two ugly smudges.

I thought of the President's new roads, and wondered what would happen if one day they should be successful. It would be a wonderful thing if a few doctors could be scattered through the country, to give the people a chance of good health, but I was very much afraid that that would be the last thing that civilisation would bring them.

Their minds and instincts would be warped first by the shoddiness of second-rate ideas, while their poor bodies would be left to go on rotting.

Graham was sub-normal again next morning, and remained so for the rest of the trip. He looked rather weak, and for the first time I was the one that was marching on ahead. Although I was in front, I was conscious of his socks slipping down, and, every now and then, I could not resist the temptation to turn round and look at them, in the same way as one's tongue touches a tender tooth from time to time to see if it is still aching.

I thought now that there was a chance that Graham might not die, and with the reaction that follows any kind of strain, the vitality of all of us sank to rock bottom and our nerves snapped. Even Amadu lost his iron self-control. The headman hit out at him over some trifling matter, and Amadu hit back. In a moment they were scratching and clawing at one another like two wild cats. The fight lasted only a minute or two, and then Amadu pulled himself together and became once more the perfect servant. But the tension hung round us in the air, and little flares of nerves and ill-temper broke out wherever two or three were gathered together. Graham and I found little to say to one another at lunch time, but as silence can sometimes become as irritating as too much talk, we gallantly searched our minds for some subject of mutual interest. Of course, the only thing we could find was food, and we stuck to that for the rest of the trip. As a matter of fact it was an entrancing subject, and even after we had stopped eating and were once again walking through the forest my mind continued to dwell on food and drink, and I longed incessantly, achingly, for smoked salmon.

It was an eight-hour walk to Gyon, the next village we were to stay at, and after a while I found tears pricking behind my eyes as I walked along muttering to myself, "I wish he'd pull his socks up. Why can't he keep his socks up?" All my tiredness and nerviness were focussed on that one point, so that in all other respects I continued to feel stolid and phlegmatic, and I never realised for a moment that I was actually extremely weary.

Only one little episode brightened our day. Tommy was drunk again and stopped to steal at every village, so that we continually had to wait for him to catch us up and show us the way. At last my cousin's patience gave out and I could see him shaking with rage. He ordered Tommy to stand in front of him, and then he swore. It was not a deliberate scolding such as had impressed our carriers at Sacrepie, but a sudden and complete loss of temper. Words and expressions I did not know existed rolled out of my cousin's mouth, stinging and lashing Tommy, till at last they penetrated through his alchoholically misty condition, and he collapsed quite suddenly, like a pricked balloon. His drunkenness left him, and he became—for a little while—a snivelling, craven little wretch, running on ahead, frightened of Graham, anxious to please, and horrible to look at. However, he was incapable of keeping this up for very long, and presently he was once again creeping off to steal a few more drinks to bolster up his self-confidence. He knew that the men despised him, and that he had lost face before us all. Presently he rejoined us again hiccoughing loudly, with his head rolling about from side to side, grinning foolishly.

At last we arrived in Gyon. It was completely deserted, for every one was out farming. There was not a soul to be seen. We sat down on our cases and waited, hour after hour, for someone to turn up. It was a dirty village. The huts were in ruins and built very low. The boys made us some tea, and we each put in one teaspoonful of whisky, which revived us considerably and seemed to us a pleasant drink. We had less than half a bottle of whisky left, and felt that we should save as much as possible for emergencies.

After three hours the villagers came back, and we were given two minute and filthy huts. Our carriers were told that there was nowhere that they could sleep and that they must be satisfied with the open palaver-house. They were very far from satisfied, for we were in leopard country and they felt sure they would be attacked. Graham's temperature was very much sub-normal. After we had taken it we asked the chief how far it was to Grand Bassa, and once again we were told that it was a seven days' march away.

Our evening meal was horrible, and it was the only occasion on which my stomach rose and revolted really strongly. As we now had neither lard nor butter our cook had cooked the chicken in palm oil. Something had apparently gone wrong with the oil that evening, for the smell was nauseating and the taste of the food utterly repellent. We played about with it for a few moments and then pretended that we were not feeling very hungry.

Our boys had a long palavar. What it was all about I could not pretend to understand, but they had apparently decided to work it out among themselves. Amadu had been chosen as judge, and he sat calmly and with the greatest dignity, facing all the men. He listened to the witnesses, he nodded his head wisely; occasionally he asked a question, but most of the time he sat silent, hearing every side. At midnight the palavar was still going on.

Early in the morning they came to Graham to appeal against judgment. He, too, listened gravely, and only I knew that he could not follow what it was all about. At last it appeared that both sides had stated their case. My cousin looked as though he were thinking it all out for a minute or two, and then for the last time he became the Great White Chief, bringing out his usual phrase with all its familiar success.

"I agree with Amadu. Palaver over."

I looked at my walking-shoes and threw them away. The soles had worn out completely and in each shoe there was a large round hole. Out of my suit-case I pulled a pair of tennis shoes with rubber soles. They were soft and comfortable, but almost unbearably hot. I could feel the stones pressing through, but my feet were hard now and no longer blistered. Graham looked better and I thought vaguely, "That's good," but did not feel anything at all. Emotionally I was as cold as a fish. I tried to think of my friends in London, but they seemed so far away that I could not concentrate on them. I knew there would be letters waiting for me in Monrovia, but the thought did not thrill me. I could think of nothing beyond the days' march. Seven days of trekking meant nothing to me; it was too big to understand. Now it was only the day that counted, the getting up at five, eating bad meals, and walking for nine endless hours. Nothing else mattered. I did not want to feel more, for I was afraid of wasting my vitality. The villages were becoming less and less attractive, and the natives more crafty, spoilt, and unpleasant. The forest was still thick, the air heavy and damp, and there were still no views. We walked mechanically, as stupid, but far less lively, as sheep being driven to market. On and on, mile after mile. In the last four weeks we had walked about three hundred and fifty miles, and now we just tramped on between the trees, while the thunder rumbled in the distance. On and on . . . on and on.

# CHAPTER XIII

WE arrived at last in a village whose name we were never quite sure of, but it sounded like Darndo; and were welcomed there by a friendly little half-caste, dressed in a pair of dirty pink-and-white-striped pyjamas.

"I see," he said, with some excitement, "that you are members of the Royal Family."

As our appearances, as far as we could tell, showed few signs of regal dignity, we were a little startled. "Why do you think that?" we asked him.

He smiled modestly. "You see," he explained, "I am a detective."

We did not contradict him, but settled down to enjoy what we could of the privileges extended to those who are born great.

The half-caste, who turned out to be the tax-collector by profession, and a detective by hobby only, left us; we saw him rummage round hectically in his hut. He returned presently with the stub of an old pencil in his hand and an expression of dismay on his face. He wanted to send a report of us down to Monrovia, he said, but, unfortunately, he could find nothing to write on. Graham most obligingly tore a few sheets of paper from his notebook and the little man was overcome with joy. For one terrible moment he had been afraid that the greatest day of his life, the never-to-be-forgotten day when he had actually shaken hands with members of the British Royal family, would pass by without bringing him that recognition from headquarters that he felt his powers of detection deserved. He wanted to do all he could for us, but at the same time we could see how he was longing to write his report, for every now and then he darted away from us, and we could see him in his hut seriously scribbling a few more words on his odd scraps of paper.

It was not possible to do a great deal for us, but whatever he could think of was swiftly and willingly accomplished. Chairs were put out in the shade and we were asked to rest.

After a while my newly acquired royal poise was momentarily shattered. The villagers were sitting in an admiring group all round us, most of them could speak English, so for the first time were able to hold some sort of conversation with them.

"I should like to drag you away to my hut," said the wit of the village, and every one laughed.

After looking at him I decided not to emulate Queen Victoria by declining to be amused, and gave him what I hoped was a gracious smile. He was a nice old man and had meant it kindly.

Oranges and lemons were brought us, baskets of glowing fruit, the first we had seen for many a long day. They had a curiously bitter taste, and we ate one after another quickly and greedily. We saw our cook watching us, a gloomy expression spreading thickly over his face. After we had eaten a good many, he drew Graham to one side, and said, "Oranges very bad. Too plenty ripe. Make massa ill."

My cousin wilted visibly at the thought of possible dysentery added to all his other troubles, and at the same time a clap of thunder rang out like a peal of mocking laughter, as if to remind us that not only was sickness chasing at our heels, but the rains as well. Graham was right, I realised, to rush to the coast.

The little tax-collector hovered round us. He arranged for us to have clean huts, and saw that the men had good food. Only one thing disturbed my serenity. A particularly repulsive-looking man attached himself to Graham and insisted on sitting at our feet. He begged my cousin to cure him, for he had great faith in the white man's medicine, and he explained with many unnecessary details that he was suffering from gonorrhœa.

For my cousin that was the last straw. He turned green, and refusing supper, went off to bed.

In the morning the air was lighter, for the storm had broken over night, and Graham felt a little better. The half-caste gave us news that gladdened our hearts and put new strength into us. Grand Bassa, quite suddenly, appeared to be only two days away. Also there was an old motor vehicle there, a lorry belonging to a Dutch Trading Co., and a road that led out about twelve miles to a village called Harlingsville. If, when we got to King Peter's Town, we sent a message ahead to the coast, the lorry could be sent to meet us and save us all a good deal of time. The news made us wild with excitement. The end was now obviously in sight.

Suddenly our hardships seemed over and we shouted

for joy. We felt friendly and happy once again, and as we set out early in the morning we took long strides and held our heads high.

Now that the end was drawing near I noticed, almost as clearly as I had done on the first day's trek, all the familiar scenes of the forest. The monkeys amused me, and the armies of ants winding their way through the bush fascinated me once more by their air of industry. The butterflies, hovering by the streams, looked like a thousand gaily coloured flower petals thrown into the air over a bride. My body was filled with a last spurt of vitality, and felt hard, and strong, and well. In imagination I blew farewell kisses to the great trees, the rough roads, and the life we were leaving behind us.

I have always hated to say good-bye, to part from the things I am used to and love. Always I like to eat my cake and have it. That whole day's march was nothing but a series of good-byes, and I wallowed, almost pleasantly, in a sea of sentimentality. Farewell to the little pink flowers, farewell to the snakes, and farewell—a long farewell—to the boredom of trekking through the forest.

It was perhaps a little early to indulge myself in all this emotion, but I was in the mood and made the most of it, for who could tell what lay in store for us the following day?

I was suffering from the reaction of the day before, and had now reached the stage where everything made me laugh. I laughed when I walked into King Peter's Town and saw it was dirty and sordid, for I somehow felt that it would be our last night in a native hut. I laughed when Graham told me that he had discovered that we would have to walk twelve hours next day to get to Harlingsville; I giggled as though he had told me a joke, and said that I did not mind at all. Weak with laughter I went into my hut and sat on my bed, and when I saw Laminah bringing in my little basin of boiled washing water, I laughed again. Laminah looked at me in amazement and then he too laughed. We laughed till the tears rolled down our cheeks, and till I suddenly discovered, to my surprise, that I was no longer laughing but crying. I put down my head on the pillow and Laminah left me alone.

I heard the whistle that Tommy always carried about with him blowing impatiently, and I went to see what he was doing. He had discovered in the village a few messengers like himself, dressed in similar blue uniforms, and had forced them to stand in what he vainly imagined was a straight line. He made them stand to attention while he lowered the Liberian flag that was fluttering in a half-hearted fashion on a decrepit flag-pole in the centre of the village. But he was in his usual state of slight intoxication, and became pettish like a child and stamped his foot, for he realised that the messengers were not taking him seriously. He kept them at it while our carriers stood round and mocked at him, till quite suddenly he lost both his temper and his interest in the whole performance, and walked away.

My cousin wrote a note to the Dutch Trading Co. in Grand Bassa asking them to send their lorry to meet us at Harlingsville, and gave it to a messenger to take down at once. Most romantically the messenger stuck the note into a cleft stick, and holding a lamp with the last of our oil in his other hand, he slipped out of the village just as it was getting dark. All through the night he would have to walk through the bush alone. Like a fairy light we could see the little lantern bobbing away from us between the trees, until it slowly disappeared.

I could hardly sleep through sheer excitement. To-morrow night, I thought, I shall sleep between white sheets. And, best of all, I should be able to sleep for twenty-four hours if I wanted to, and no one would wake me at five o'clock to tell me to get up. It sounded too good to be true, and as a matter of fact it was.

We got up at four, and Graham said that nothing in the world would make him spend another night on the road to Harlingsville. We walked rapidly, a cross-country race of unknown length. Even the men were excited, and we all pressed forward as though lashed by whips, driven on by my cousin's feverish impatience. We hurried, feeling neither the heat nor weariness, and thinking nothing except: " We must get to Harlingsville, we must get to Harlingsville."

After a while we had a little break, and such a pleasant one that for half an hour I relaxed completely and forgot everything in the deep contentment I felt in my surroundings. For we had come to another mission and were welcomed by the German missionary and his wife. I cannot remember anything about the man, but the picture of the woman lies enshrined in my heart. She was fat, large and kind, and her straight greyish hair was pulled with great force back from her red face and pinned into a tight little bun behind. She looked exactly the kind of picture that springs to the mind when one tries to imagine an old-fashioned, middle-class German

*Hausfrau.* She was perfect in every detail. It was almost as if she had dressed the part for a joke to go to a party, and she remembered everything, down to the black woollen stockings. But her heart was as large as her body and she seemed to exude kindness from every pore. She gave us iced fruit drinks and delicious gingerbread, and provided —ever true to her character—little paper serviettes so that we might delicately wipe our rough red fingers. And suddenly she nearly made me weep, for she put her hand softly on my head and said, "Mein armes Kind," exactly as my mother used to say to me when as a child I was feeling sad. And I realised that what I wanted more than anything was to be petted and spoilt a little bit and to be made a fuss of. When I wanted to thank her as we said good-bye I could hardly say a word in case my voice should tremble, for since the day before I could never be sure of my mood from one moment to another.

Harlingsville was only another six hours' walk, they told us, and then added that they thought the lorry at Grand Bassa had broken down a few months before, and that we would probably have to walk the other two hours to the coast.

There was nothing to be done about it, but Graham looked very ill and I could not understand how he was going to keep on.

We raced on once more, and suddenly we were out of the forest and on to broad, open country. I was used by this time to being surrounded by trees, and at first experienced none of that splendid freedom which I had expected I would feel, but felt instead curiously conspicuous and unsheltered; a little shy, as if I had suddenly cast aside my clothes.

And now "civilisation" was beginning—a few badly built houses with broken and rusty tin roofs, a few half-castes lying asleep in the dust with a bottle of cane juice at their sides, a woman slapping her child in shrill irritation.

I turned a corner and there stood the lorry.

It was wonderful. It was like waking up as a very small child on Christmas morning and finding that Father Christmas really *had* been. I was dumb with joy and wonder.

Not so our carriers. They had never seen anything like it before, and were examining it from every side, chattering like magpies. Our boys, delighted to be placed in such an obviously superior position, explained to them a trifle smugly what it was all about. It was some time before they could understand that the lorry would actually carry us all with all our cases, and with no physical effort on our part, the whole way down to the coast. Neither had they any idea what the coast was, for none of them had ever seen the sea and they were now waiting impatiently for the mystery to be divulged. They were quite right to feel amazed. It was the most astonishing sensation to be sitting still while the trees and houses slipped by. No effort, no effort at all. That drive in the old lorry as it rattled along with its cargo of thirty-two human beings, crushed one upon the other, was one of the most utterly satisfying experiences I have ever had.

We arrived in Bassa Town only just in time. The one white inhabitant was about to leave the town. He was the storekeeper and was closing up his shop through lack of business. The first thing he did was to put a large glass of iced beer into our hands, but to my sorrow I did not enjoy it as much as I thought I would. As so very often happens, anticipation was a far, far better thing than realisation.

Graham paid off the carriers, while the storekeeper impressed on each one that he should go away as quickly as possible. They were too innocent to be safe in the town as long as they had money. They would be robbed and the police too would take away all they had with many fictitious fines and taxes. The men looked bewildered, for they felt lost now without Graham, who had been their father for so long. They did not know the way home, they said, and asked if it were possible to go along the seashore. The storekeeper told them to hurry inland as quickly as possible, for they were in danger as long as they were near the coast, and no one was safe without a gun on the lonely parts of the shore. They were like children and stood huddled together, looking odd now in their primitive garments.

Later we took a little walk through the town and I saw that they had all got drunk, not in a pleasant, dreamy way on palm wine, but roughly and noisily on cheap cane juice. I went back to the shop so that I could not see what we had done to them. That their money would soon be spent was obvious, for the townspeople were already upon them like a flock of vultures, picking them clean. The police, too, were taking some of them away to the police station to make sure that they too would get their share before it was too late. I hoped sincerely that all their money would be gone by the morning so that they would hurry back to their homes and to the lives that suited them.

"Fresh beef," announced the storekeeper proudly, as he helped us during supper. "I'm glad I managed to get hold of some for you. It's not often that we have such luxuries."

No one could say that we had been spoilt recently by good food, or that we were over-fastidious about what we ate, but as I chewed and chewed at a rubber-like bit of meat, tougher even than the chicken we were used to, I was overcome with wonder at the man sitting so contentedly at the head of the table.

"Good, isn't it?" he said, helping himself to some more.

I swallowed a large bit whole. "Excellent," I said.

For years he had been alone in this little town, and now that the shop had failed he was moving to join up with the store in Monrovia. Moving to the capital, he called it proudly, thrilled to be going to the centre of things, to be one of thirty white people instead of by himself.

We had imagined that we would probably be stranded in Grand Bassa for a week before a boat would come to take us away. And "Twenty-four hours' sleep," I said to myself happily as I got into bed.

I seemed hardly to have fallen asleep when I felt myself being shaken fiercely. I opened my eyes and beheld an agitated Laminah. It was still very early.

"Go away," I said.

"Missis get up. Plenty fine boat. Go quick, quick, quick Monrovia."

Graham came in to tell me to get dressed. A small boat was making its maiden voyage to Monrovia with a load of politicians. If we were in time we could go with them.

I hurried as much as I could, and was soon scrambling after Graham down to the quay.

It was a very small boat indeed, and looked completely unseaworthy. The storekeeper had come to see us off and was now begging us not to trust ourselves on to such a frail vessel. It was already piled high with black men, at least one hundred and fifty of them, who tried to stop us coming on board, screaming out with great truth that there was no room. The captain apparently was determined to make money while he could, for the boat was so flimsy that it seemed likely that her first voyage would also be her last. He somehow managed to squeeze us in with our boys, called out that anyone who moved would be put in irons, blew a little whistle, and gave the order to put off.

The politicians on board were members of the Opposition who were going to Monrovia to stage demonstrations for the forthcoming presidential elections. Being of the Opposition they thought apparently that they were expected to oppose anything they could, on every possible occasion. They opposed the captain when he shouted out orders to the engineer down below; they opposed everything my cousin said; and they noisily opposed each other. The uproar was deafening and cane juice circulated freely.

"Don't move!" screamed the captain every time anyone sank to the floor overcome by drunkenness. The boat would quiver and sway over to the side until by a miracle it would right itself again.

I fell asleep, and when I woke up a few hours later nearly every one was drunk. The tumult and the shouting had died down and was only revived spasmodically. The politicians, sitting on the deck packed closely together, had for the greater part fallen asleep. The captain looked as if he too had indulged in a few drinks, and I was glad, for the sake of my peace of mind, that I could not see the engineer. The boat chugged on its staggering way hour after hour. The sun beat down, and on every side I was pressed in by intoxicated politicians. Some were groaning slightly, for the sun and the cane juice were making them feel sick, and some were snoring rather noisily in their sleep.

At last we reached Monrovia. Like most small tropical towns it looked enchanting from the sea. The sun on the green trees and yellow sands made it look fairy-like and delicate; and hope springing eternally in my human breast murmured to me, "What an enchanting place."

I shall go to bed very, very early, I decided, and explore the town the next day, when I am feeling fresher.

We arrived at the house we were to stay at and found there was a party going on. Before we had time to tidy up, drinks were thrust into our hands. No one seemed surprised to see us, or asked about our trip. Most of the people present had lived for many, many years in Monrovia, but I never came across anyone who had been farther up-country than two days' trek. It was one of the subjects that was simply not interesting. As a matter of fact no one spoke very much. It seemed too hot to do anything but drink.

After supper I murmured, "I'm afraid I must go to bed. I'm a little tired."

"Nonsense," shouted every one. "You can't spoil the party. Have another drink."

At twelve o'clock I gathered up courage again and said, "I must go to bed."

"It's far too early," shouted every one, reviving for a moment from the heavy drowsiness into which we had all sunk. "Have another drink."

I did not want another drink, but I was too tired to argue about anything, and I let them pour it out. That little breath of vitality soon died in every one and we sank back into a state of complete listlessness.

It was incredibly hot and sticky, and the air seemed heavier than we had known it on our trek. It was not only my tiredness that made me feel it. Every one in the room was exhausted with it. I had chosen a place by the window so that I could pour away my drinks from time to time and so avoid further uncomplimentary remarks being directed against my lack of party spirit.

At two o'clock I pulled myself together. "I'm going to bed," I said firmly. "Good night."

Refusing all drinks, and in spite of the wails that followed my progress from the room that I might be breaking up the party, I left them. They were kind, hospitable people, but the moment had come when nothing in the world could keep me awake any longer. I went to bed and blew out my light.

The adventure was over. I was back in civilisation.

## CHAPTER XIV

I HATED every moment of my time in Monrovia. I was tired, but, what was far worse, I was bored. During every minute, every second of the days I spent there, my soul was overpowered by such an appalling state of boredom as I hope never to experience again.

The weather, with the rainy season just about to break, 'was ghastly, and drained every spark of vitality out of the body. Graham strangely enough revived slightly, but I felt completely exhausted. Out of the thirty white people living in Monrovia nine went down with various illnesses while I was there.

I longed to sleep, but our endless social duties made it impossible for me to rest properly. I pined for a long soft drink, but it was one of the most difficult things to get hold of. Gin would be poured generously into the lemonade with which we took our quinine in the morning, and when I tried to explain to the boy that I would like a non-alcoholic drink, he smiled understandingly, went away, and presently returned with a whisky-and-soda. The rest of the morning was spent going round from house to house drinking beer. After lunch it was too hot to do anything even if we had been capable of it by that time, and later in the evening the endless parties began again till three or four in the morning. I was shrieked at every time I asked for some plain lemonade or a glass of water, and told that I was spoiling the party, and I was too tired to argue or to be amused at the situation. I sat most of the time glum and silent, a difficult and tiresome guest. I must have poured gallons of gin and sticky, sweet *crème de menthe* out of the windows of the various rooms in which we were entertained.

There was nothing to do. I tried to bathe, but before I got up to my knees in the water I could feel the currents pulling at me so strongly that it needed all my strength to get back to the shore, and I was asked not to do it again. Once a week the men congregated together to shoot at bottles, and once a week they had a billiard party. Otherwise there were no amusements. There were no books to read, for in that climate they soon rotted or else were eaten by ants. There was no golf course and no horses. The white inhabitants were members of every nationality and class, drawn together into an unnaturally close and intimate life, with no distractions, no amusements, and no real work to help them through their days of exile. It was a lost and dreary corner of the world where every day appeared as a vast and shadeless desert that had to be crossed before night could again bring a few hours of sweet forgetfulness. There was nothing to do except drink. Once a fortnight the mail boat from England would call, bringing letters and frozen beef to the exiles, and a little flutter of excitement could be felt. The letters read, there would be nothing new for another fortnight. Nothing that could possibly happen. Even the whispered scandals could never be very exciting, for they too were deadly monotonous. I was tired, I was bored, and I did not want to drink. The days seemed endless.

Monrovia was a ramshackle town, with most of the houses in a state of semi-decay. The President's palace was the most impressive building, but its dignity was perhaps slightly impaired by the sight of His Excellency's suits, hung out to air on the balconies.

The streets were rough and overgrown with weeds. There were telegraph poles dotted about the town, but they were only one sign among many of ambitious plans that had lived a few months and then died in sickly and under-nourished infancy. The post office was a wooden loft into which one climbed by an old ladder. Altogether it was a sad town and seemed dead except on those occasions when political demonstrations, with the help of cane juice, filled the streets with excited people and the air with shrieks.

If I am giving an over-dreary picture of the town, I hope I shall be forgiven. Perhaps in the mood I was in nothing would have appealed to me. The seven wonders of the world, the harbour of Rio de Janeiro by moonlight, Paris in spring-time, might all have had their radiance dimmed for my eyes at that moment. I was tired and my soul was dead and incapable of being resurrected till my body had been revived with good food, baths and a manicure.

Occasionally at rather stiff dinner-parties we met the members of the Liberian Cabinet and their wives. In startling contrast to most of the white guests at these parties all the Ministers we met in Monrovia remained completely sober, very often refusing to drink anything at all. Conversation during dinner was not conspicuous for its sparkle and vivacity, and many and long were the pauses that crept in, in spite of all our nervous attempts at bright chatter. Agitatedly we would throw the ball to one another, but it seemed always to be a ball of exceptional weight and impossible to keep in the air, and soon—very soon—it would fall crashing to the ground and lie in splinters at our feet. There was almost a rhythm about it. The silence that followed each crash was no silence of repose. It meant for all of us a hectic search into the corners of our minds for something, however dim and dull, that could be dragged out to cover the next few moments. Unlike the jovial President, or the dramatic Col. Davis, most of the Ministers were too earnest, too shy and serious, to feel at their ease at these parties. My sympathy was with them. There was an absence of ease and geniality, and we all visibly writhed in agony.

The Secretary of the Treasury, however, was different. He was a well-dressed young man, with large sad eyes. He was, I suppose, the most highly cultured member of the Government and had travelled to Europe several times. He had an admiration for culture and learning and the arts, and it was rather sad that he had so few opportunities to follow up his interests. He asked my cousin and I to tea at his house, and was dressed for the occasion in somewhat studied Bohemianism: a flowing tie, a careful carelessness in his dress; so that we realised that we were in for an artistic party of some sort. We were right.

"I thought we would have a little music," he said, and led us into a small and exceedingly stuffy music-room.

He sang to us, soft sentimental songs composed by the President himself. Our host's voice was sweet, but unfortunately was not as easy to hear as we would have liked, for the piano was so completely out of tune and harsh owing to the climate that it was only on very rare occasions that a note or two of the song could reach us. Song followed song in rapid succession. Graham and I sat stiffly on very hard chairs and murmured our pleasure from time to time. The songs were all of a sugary sweetness and expressed slightly Victorian sentiments. The party left an indelible record on my mind. It will never, I feel sure, fade from my memory.

Otherwise we did nothing. Every now and then a rumour would reach us that a boat was expected, but a few hours later it would be denied again.

Our boys were still hovering round us, ready to serve us to the last minute. They seemed heartbroken at the thought that we would have to part with them at Freetown; we were so used to one another now and knew each other's little ways. We gave them all our old and broken things. Amadu accepted everything with dignity, but Laminah danced round me begging incessantly for everything I possessed.

"I think I'll take my shorts back to England," I said to Graham. "I could wear them in the country."

It was certainly a foolish idea, for I had never liked them at all, but I was considerably surprised when I found Graham extremely upset at the suggestion.

"No, you can't," he said furiously, and told me with all the wealth of phrase at his command exactly what I looked like in them. It was worse even than I had imagined, and hurriedly and humbly I gave the shorts to Laminah.

We waited. We drank. I never went to bed till the early hours of the morning. I think my cousin was as bored as I was, but his manners were better and he did not show it so much. I admired but found it was beyond my strength to emulate him. The days crept by.

I thought of the moonlight nights and the sweet music of the harps and the sudden frantic rush to the coast when the days had glided into one another with the rapidity and smoothness of a dream. Memory, the kindest faculty we possess, was already curing all the bruises we had received, and leaving as highlights in our minds only the joys and pleasures of our trip.

"Farewells should be sudden," said Byron. How right he was. The play was over, but the curtain had got stuck and we were left on the stage with nothing to do. I had said my farewells long ago in the forest and now wanted to leave the whole comedy behind me. This dragging out of the end was inartistic and spoiling the balance of the whole thing. It was sad, I felt, that one could never rely on life to construct its scenes without the inevitable anticlimax.

At last a small cargo boat arrived with room for us. I stumbled on board, went straight to my cabin, and fell asleep. I woke for a little while when we called at Freetown—long enough to bid a sad farewell to our boys, and to go to one or two parties and once again have innumerable, unwanted drinks pressed into my hand.

As soon as I could I escaped back to the boat, and presently was lying in a bath, up to the neck in clean, warm water. But this slow return to civilisation was a drab, unsatisfactory business. The bath water was salty and left me feeling hot and sticky. Nothing was working out as I had hoped it would.

The days—indescribably dreary—passed by like a slow-motion picture. Soon we left behind the burning sunshine and plunged into storms and fogs. My only warm dress was filthy, the rats had eaten my stockings, and my mackintosh was torn beyond repair. I found I was tired of being dirty, and all day long I shivered with cold. I was incapable somehow of looking forward to the future with any excitement.

The days crept by till we finally got to Dover. At four o'clock in the morning we were turned off the boat. It was raining and a bitterly cold April morning. Graham and I, silent and depressed, sat on our boxes in the custom house, waiting for an official to come and let us through.

At last the time came for me to say good-bye to Graham, for he was staying on in Dover, and I returned to sit on my boxes till a train could take me to London.

Lonely and pathetic I sat and waited, a tired, ragged waif in an old mackintosh, no stockings, and a strange thing on my head that had once been a hat.

The rain poured down, the wind whistled round me, and I felt alone in the world.

"Come and 'ave some coffee, miss," said a porter to me. "Train won't be due for some time yet."

I got up and followed him silently. There was a fire, and the coffee was hot.

"Wherever 'ave you been to?" asked the porter.

I looked at my few possessions: a native harp, some swords and daggers. I was warm now and suddenly the world seemed a happier place.

'It was worth it," I said.